# I'M HIGHLY
# PERCENT
# SURE

# I'M HIGHLY PERCENT SURE

## CAROLINE A. WANGA

AMISTAD
*An Imprint of HarperCollinsPublishers*

Lavette
Books

Career Chart on page 37 published by permission of CNBC.

Photograph on page 64 published by permission of Target Corporation.

Introvert Illustration on page 124 published by permission of Wanga Woman LLC and Summer Koide.

HarperCollins books may be purchased for educational, business, or sales promotional use. For information, please email the Special Markets Department at SPsales@harpercollins.com.

FIRST EDITION

*Designed by Janet Evans-Scanlon*
*Introvert illustration on page 124 by Summer Koide*
*Space break ornaments © WinWin/stock.adobe.com*
*Texture on title page and contents page © Miubewa/stock.adobe.com*
*Laughing emoji on page 167 © Denis Gorelkin/Shutterstock*
*Eyes emoji on page 168 © obitoclast/Shutterstock*
*Shrugging emoji on page 168 © Valentina Vectors/Shutterstock*

Library of Congress Cataloging-in-Publication Data has been applied for.

ISBN 978-0-06-336038-9

25 26 27 28 29 LBC 5 4 3 2 1

This book is dedicated to Karton's wife; KJ, Piper, and Skylar's mom; a conversationalist who punctuates all interactions with laughter; and a person I don't like but deeply love: Barkue (6 Bics) Tubman-Zawolo. My sis-tah, your dedication to ushering people into the places and spaces designed for them is your divine purpose and eternal legacy. You have been a staunch regulator of my energy (to stay healthy) but also a disciplinarian of my defiance (to propel my purpose). So I stand forever grateful and indebted to your self-lessness and grit that are helping me step into this new season of my life.

"Asante Sana, Dada."

—The Giraffe, aka Sergeant at Arms
of the Serengeti

#WakeUpAndSayAmen
#ListenWithYourEyes

# CONTENTS

# FOREWORD BY BRIAN CORNELL
## Defiant Pursuit of Purpose

Caroline and I used to joke that, at first glance, we don't seem to share much in common.

She was born in Kenya. I grew up in Queens. My closet contains blue sports coats and slacks. She's known to sport blue lipstick and sequins. Caroline commands the attention of any room she enters and is among the most dynamic and captivating speakers to ever step onstage. I'm more reserved—and, over the years, have been asked to deliver speeches right after her, which I wouldn't advise for anyone.

But to know Caroline is to know the meaning of authenticity. Not the buzzword but the genuine embrace of everything that makes us similar and the qualities that make us distinct.

In these pages, Caroline shares an anecdote about the first time we sat side by side in a boardroom, the final bastion of formal business attire. She wore bold, colorful sneakers and recounts being surprised that, as CEO, I'd compliment her nontraditional choice in footwear. Caroline might be the only one who remembers that. What I, and the rest of the board, remembered was the strength of the strategy she presented that day.

It was the summer of 2014, and I had just moved cross-country to start my role as Target's CEO. The business faced complex challenges, but I was drawn to Target's iconic brand and reputation as an academy company that attracts and develops world-class leaders. Caroline, recently elevated to Target's top DE&I role, was one of them. She welcomed me with tremendous energy and wide-open arms. And she let me know I had joined a team with a special culture and deeply rooted values.

We soon discovered we share a competitive spirit and team-focused mindset, dating back to our years as student-athletes. She's a relentlessly curious, lifelong learner and an active listener—traits I strive to practice daily. We favor progress over perfection. We bonded over how we're both dedicated parents.

Caroline and I also share nonlinear career paths. I didn't set out to become CEO of a $100 billion retailer. It never entered the consideration set for a teenager who was cutting lawns and washing Tropicana trucks to pay for sports equipment and, eventually, college tuition. I'd imagine that chief executive of an iconic media brand hadn't been in Caroline's sights as a single mother interning at Target's distribution center in Texas either.

Caroline's journey illuminates what's possible for those who identify, articulate, and commit wholeheartedly to what she describes as a "defiant pursuit of purpose." Very few successful leaders I've met are motivated by a quest for material wealth or prestigious titles. Visionaries like Caroline set bold ambitions, are guided by consistent values, and embrace the unexpected opportunities—and obstacles—that life presents along the way.

At Target, Caroline built on our culture of care and belonging, which has helped our business grow for decades. She introduced even more sophistication to our work, reinforcing the power of transparent reporting and amplifying diverse perspectives. She pushed me and our leadership team to ensure our aspirations were backed by action.

By modeling authenticity every day, Caroline inspires those around her to bring their full selves—and their boldest thinking—to work. Caroline calls this a "cycle of upliftment." I'd call it "competitive advantage." As basketball legend Bill Walton recounted from his days on the court with Coach John Wooden: "When everyone thinks alike, no one thinks." And in the fast-paced, intensely competitive world of retail, innovative thinking is vital. If you're not moving forward, you've already fallen behind.

Nothing propels a business forward like hundreds of thousands of team members applying their diverse ideas and experiences to how we deliver on a shared purpose. Today it's why Target's growth trajectory is measured not by months or years but generations.

In 2020, when Caroline called me to say she had been offered the job as CEO of Essence, I was sad to see her go. But I was eager to see her apply the full strength and influence of her purpose to a once-in-a-lifetime opportunity.

We talked about which elements would feel familiar and which would be different. Some business metrics would carry over from retail to media. Others wouldn't. Decisions from the CEO seat would require a great deal of personal judgment. When she asked my advice, I said, "Sometimes you just need to listen to your intuition and trust your gut."

No one gets it right 100 percent of the time. And the story Caroline shares here proves that—even when you're "highly percent sure" and following your North Star—the path is rarely well lit or easy to navigate.

But I offered Caroline that guidance because I was confident that through decades of living in defiant pursuit of her purpose, she had developed an exceptional personal compass. And her journey, like the one that Target's team remains on today, demonstrates the boundless potential for those who press forward unwaveringly.

*Brian Cornell*
Chair and CEO of Target

# PREFACE

I am on a video conference call. I've been talking about myself for nearly an hour. Not difficult. I am an expert on the subject. I am engaged. I am listening, but the conversation has shifted to discussing my book's marketing strategy and release. As the conversation continues, I am silent. My head rests on my hand, partially covering my face, as I shrink to the bottom of the screen. La Juana Whitmore, CEO of WangaWoman LLC, can see I am becoming increasingly uncomfortable. I want to get off this call and get as far away from the naked intimacy of this fully uncomfortable moment as possible. Why?

While I am used to talking to groups about myself, it is different when groups are talking to me about me. It is the difference between being the product versus the vessel. In this case—on the video call—the conversation about marketing my book has made me the product, which is uncomfortable. And now I'm trying to figure out what to do with this dissonance.

Warning: I curse as a part of my self-compassion plan. (More on that plan later.) It helps me not make other bad decisions. I never had a desire to write a damn book. The first reason I didn't want to write a book is because I didn't think my impact would translate well when written down. People react to my story through my delivery: the sound, the cadence, and the ethos of my voice. My response to this energy around me about writing a book—which is primarily energy external to me—has always been that it loses something. I often reject anything that causes my message to lose impact.

So I've resolved to deliver stories verbally to protect the impact of my message. Secondly, I am perfectly comfortable talking about myself and what my story can do for others. I value the immediate impact on the person listening when I speak to or interact with in person. I know how people are impacted, because after I speak, whether live or via a posted comment, they confirm that what I've shared makes a difference in how they exist in the world. I gather their sentiment by asking a very simple question . . . What resonated with you? My decision to write this book is tied to what I believe is a necessary step in my journey to fulfilling my purpose by showing up for myself and you, and maintaining my comfort is less important than your progress.

I am self-aware enough to know that my discomfort can torpedo something like writing this book. Usually, it happens by shrinking, hiding, or self-deprecation to the point of sabotage. To ensure I delivered this book, I had to mitigate self-sabotage. So I assigned myself one job on this book journey—tell my story and leave the rest of the process to everyone but me. So thank you to all those who played the roles I couldn't so that we could deliver the contents of this story to all those for whom it is necessary.

# I'M HIGHLY PERCENT SURE

# Abashitsetse [A-ba-shee-sese]

You are probably trying to figure out how to pronounce the name of this chapter, and you will probably be trying to figure out how to pronounce the next chapter too. So to help y'all out, I'm going to let my daddy, aka Dr. Lucas Wanga, explain this chapter, "Abashitsetse," which is the name for the father of a Bwibo. I'll see y'all in the next chapter. Enjoy!

The story I'm going to give you is about Caroline Wanga and her ancestors. Where they came from, where they are right now, and where they are going, including the Kenya kingdom issue. The story starts thousands of years ago. It's not a story that you will find in many European writings. It's a story that precedes the European biblical time, and it's a story that has nothing to do with the European biblical story. The ancestors of Caroline Auma Wanga trace their beginnings to Misri.

Now, Misri is the present-day Egypt. We know it as "Misri," and almost every African comes from Misri. Anyway, this is about five thousand, seven thousand years ago. In African terms, the word "Egypt" is more of a European terminology. But it was there before the Europeans came and named it "Egypt." Things like the pyramids and the pharaohs are things from Misriland before it became Egypt. This is history from five thousand to seven thousand years ago.

Both of Caroline's parents trace their ancestry to the same area. I am Bantu from Egypt, and Caroline's mother is Nilot from Egypt. Luos are Nilots. Caroline's mother is a Luo. I'm Luyiah Bantu. Bantu is generally genealogical. Luyiah is a sect of the Bantu group. The Bantu group occupies most of eastern Africa, southern Africa, and western Africa. The Luos occupy most of Sudan, part of Uganda, Kenya, a little bit of Tanzania. I'm Luyiah of the Bantu genealogy.

About seven thousand years ago, the ancestors of Caroline Wanga, the Wangas, left Misri and traveled through western Sudan to the area now called Cameroon. They lived there for a while, then traveled across Sudan into the present-day Ethiopia. They lived in Ethiopia for some time, then moved back to Sudan. They then followed the Nile into Bunyoro and then settled into Buganda. Here in Buganda, they established the Buganda Kingdom about two thousand years ago. In the nineteenth century, meaning 1800s AD—remember, we are coming from seven thousand years ago, so we are now in AD—due to Samiai-related squabbles, a man by the name of Muwanga III split from the Buganda Kingdom and traveled through Samia. He settled in Leila in Maseno, near Kisumu in Kenya. Maseno is near the place presently called Kisumu. Okay. Now I have a little context that I need to add on now that I should have said at the beginning. All this time, there is no Kenya. It's just land, barren land. There's no Uganda, there is no Kenya, there is no Ethiopia. All those are European creations that come much later. So I'm not talking about Kenya. I can talk about the area and then designate it by telling you what's there now.

I can say they settled in a place that is now known as Leila, but this is near Lake Nyanza. Lake Nyanza is what you may know as Lake Victoria. All this time, I'm not talking of Lake Victoria or any of the present names that you know are artificial—they're European-made, which has a lot to do later with colonialism. In the eighteenth century, due to family-related squabbles, Muwanga III split from the Buganda kingdom, traveled through Samia, and settled at Leila in Maseno, which is near Lake Victoria or near present-day Kisumu. His son Muwanga moved to Tiriki, now called western Kenya. He left Tiriki in an attempt to go back to his ancestral home in Buganda. He was making a turnaround because he was tired of moving. He was kind of lost; he just wanted to get back home again. People do that most of the time. Exhausted, he ended up in Muima's home in Imanga. Poor and poorly treated, he then left where he had been housed, and then moved to Emurabe, and then to Eshikulu, where he established his first home in the present Muwanga area. We're getting home now. I want to make an interjection here that this Eshikulu is only two miles away from my present home. That's how close I am to the issue. Not only that, but as it will come to show, I am of the Wanga clan.

Muwanga continued to establish other homes in the area, like Elureko. He also established a home in Ejinja. Matungu is where he was buried, and it's now the center of the Wanga kingdom. So the story that I've just given is a narration of the people who eventually ended up becoming the Wanga kingdom. I've given you their routes through present Cameroon, Sudan, Ethiopia, Uganda, and finally Kenya. In Kenya, they also moved around, and finally this kingdom settled down in Ematungu.

My ancestry is Bantu. Caroline's mother comes from the Luo

community, so her mother is Luo, of Nilotic ancestry. "Nilotic" simply means that they came down through the River Nile from Missouri. So Nilotic has reference to the River Nile. The Luo people trace their ancestry from Misri, which is Egypt, around the same time, five thousand or seven thousand years ago. They moved from Misri through the Nile Valley or the River Nile Valley and first settled in the area you call South Sudan, then moved farther south to the shores of Nyanza Lake or Lake Nyanza (Lake Victoria). They occupied the whole of the northern part of Lake Nyanza, including South Nyanza. Similar history but a slightly different name and a different travel route. These routes did not take a day. It was not like they started and ended the next day. This took thousands of years, meaning they reached a place, and they lived there for a while. I mean, where "a while" could be several hundred years. And for reasons that I don't know, they started to move to the next place. And so five to seven thousand years they are traveling, and finally, they are in a place we now call Kenya.

The Wanga kingdom begins with Nabongo Wanga. Nabongo was going to be elevated to king. So by saying "Nabongo Wanga," I'm saying "King Wanga." The only caveat is that rarely does that appear in most European writing. We are not even called kings. That's English. Nabongo Wanga in Tiriki, present-day western Kenya. Wanga left Tiriki in an attempt to get back to his ancestral land, which was Buganda. Exhausted, he ended up in Muima's home in Imanga.

Imanga is four miles south of Mumias, which is the big town in Wanga. It's next to Matungu, where the kings are buried. So this is the center of the Wanga. There's a center for the kingdom, which is Matungu, but there is also a center for the Wanga, which is Mumias. That's their city. Wanga was mistreated in Muima's home, and after, his brothers and cousins arrived. His people went after him in Muima's home. He was a king, and he got into somebody's home who was also a leader of his group. So there was a cultural conflict, meaning kings could not be getting into each other's homes. So Muima was rejecting him, saying, "You, as a ruler, should not enter my home." So once his cousins and brothers showed up, Wanga then moved out of Muima's home to Emurabe, and then to Eshikulu, where he established his first home in the Wanga area. This is only a mile or so from my home. So all it is is a story that I've heard over and over and over again from almost everybody. Wanga continued to establish other homes in the area, like El Reco, which is El Reco (Mumias), Ejinja, and Matungu. The cultural center of the Wanga kingdom, Matungu, and the Abawanga people.

Now I'm getting to the growth and development of the Wanga kingdom. Wanga started with hard work. He grew enough grain for food and for resale, and, by that time, they were using the barter system. There were no dollars and no shillings, meaning there was no paper money or any money of any form. You grew crops or you had cattle, and you did an exchange. Barter system. In the process, he acquired plenty of livestock and women and children. Those are part of the cultural values. Land, livestock, women, and children. Which made him very wealthy and famous. Given the fact that he was a na-bongo, meaning he was "king" in European terms, he commanded quite a lot of respect.

He used his wealth and power to intimidate his other neighboring communities and community members and subjected them to his own rule. He waged war. Meaning, well, he waged war with his neighbors and further subdued them under his rule. He waged war because he was very powerful and wanted more power. This was somebody who was a king already, and using his wealth and what have you, he started to wage war with his neighbors and neighboring communities in search of power. This process of waging war to subdue his neighbors continued within, with his successors in the kingdom. The kingdom used mercenaries like the Maasai community, and later, even later on, they used the colonial British to do their mercenary work. Mercenaries are hired soldiers. Those mercenaries were Maasai. Wanga was not a Maasai, but Maasai liked war. So he was hiring warriors to come and fight for him.

One of his successors, Mumia, hired colonial British people with guns to fight for him. These were colonizers. To further anger and subdue his opponents. Using the colonial power as mercenaries to gain territory, he came to be viewed by his enemies as collaborating with the British colonial rule or colonial rulers to harass neighbors and acquire their territories. I mean, snatching cattle and women and children. So he became a menace, to the point where the kingdom grew at the peril of his neighbors or neighboring communities.

He ended up occupying almost twenty-two other neighboring communities, fighting with them, overpowering them, and taking their land, and therefore, he was even using mercenaries to do that. That was not unusual. That was how wars were fought. That was how people who wanted to expand used different tactics to do what they had to do to gain what they had to gain. So, confusing as it is, I just want you to understand that there he was, using mercenaries to enhance his strength of conquering others. To the extent that he even used the British. He therefore looked like he was a collaborator with the British colonizers. But it wasn't about slavery. The British in East Africa were not necessarily after slaves. They were after other things. The British wanted to extend their invasion into Uganda. And they were willing to collaborate with him so as for him to give them leeway into Uganda. Remember, we spoke of Buganda earlier. Buganda is in Uganda.

Muwanga quarreled with his brothers and then left for Kenya. So he's related to the people of Buganda. Remember, when Muwanga left Tiriki, he was trying to get back to Buganda. That was his ancestral home area, only he became stuck somewhere in Kenya, in Muima's home, which is next to my home. So his kingdom was very much connected with the kingdom of Buganda. There was a little trick here, whether the Wangas were behaving like colonizers, or they were just taking advantage. They continued to do this for several years. To the extent that the Maasai only left Mumia in 1956.

Maasai had been given a territory to occupy, so when they were doing all their raids and helping the kingdom, the kingdom gave them land to live on. But they are a group of a different nationality, so eventually, when the wars had ended, they saw no need to stay around—they moved on to their territory somewhere else.

Wanga kingdom happened to have been in an area in which the British saw an advantage. The British needed the Wanga kingdom to help them go to Uganda, to colonize and do other things and find the River Nile and what have you. Their quest was to get to Buganda, to learn the source of the River Nile. When the British were looking for a way to get to Buganda, they found the kings of Muwanga were related to the kings of Buganda, and they tried to use them as a way to Uganda. The king, on the other hand, told the British he would help them if they helped him expand his kingdom. So that was where the mercenary issue came in. The British agreed to help him expand his territory, and the king agreed to help them go to Uganda, which was Buganda. The British wanted to discover the source of the River Nile. For thousands of years, the River Nile has been one of the most renowned and most respected rivers in the area because it flows from the interior of Africa to the European Mediterranean Sea. And there was a curiosity around finding the source of this river. The source of the River Nile is in Jinja, Uganda. The river flows from Lake Victoria through a known little town called Jinja. So you can see the connection between the British interest and the Wanga kingdom's interest. The Wanga kingdom's interest was to expand territory and power. The British interest was for the Wangas to help them get to Uganda. To find the source of the River Nile; it also ended with the colonizing of Uganda. So they negotiated. The British agreed to leave the Wanga alone as long as they helped them. But the Wanga kingdom was saying, "If you want us to help you get to Uganda, we want to gain more territory." They had signed a treaty in which they agreed they would not colonize Wangaland. As a result, we don't have white farmers in Wangaland, even today. Wangaland was never occupied. As a result, you have the land, you have the people, you likely survive. That's how the Wanga kingdom survived. It is still there. It is still called Wangaland, and the kingdom is still there.

After Kenya regained independence and took over from the colonial British government, the Wanga kingdom was reduced to the cultural leadership of the Abawanga and Abashitsetse. Wangaland was reduced to just one ruling clan. The other clans that they had captured were receded. Now they had no power over all these other clans, but they still had some sort of cultural leadership within the Abashitsetse clan, who are the originators of the Wanga kingdom and maintain a sense of rulership because they're the original. The ruling clan is still the original.

The British have no direct rule. Kenya is completely independent. Military, police, everything. However, I can say the British still have some influence, which is more or less indirect and not powerful. For example, some of the land that they used to occupy and own when they were colonizers, they still own either directly or indirectly.

Kenyans have the majority rule, but some of the Europeans or the British still have shares in what they used to own before but with minority shares. Although Kenyans have majority shares in some countries, if you're not a citizen, you can't own majority shares of land.

They also still have British bases and other military bases, just like America. Even the US has a base in Kenya. The bases are mainly to protect their interests. The present Wanga king is called Peter Mumia II. The truth is, although the kingdom solicited help from some in the British colonial government, it was a process that was not encouraged by the rest of the colonial regime. It later backfired and was abandoned. It resulted in the colonial system reducing the kingdom's power to mere chiefdoms.

The current king has no Kenyan governmental administrative responsibilities or functions. Here is a king who has no power, no duties, and no responsibilities, yet, to a little extent, the government collects taxes and pays him. Sort of like in England. But it creates the funny irony that the government, which has nothing to do with the monarch, still pays the monarch. Remember, the Wanga king, or King Peter Mumia II, is not a government official. The king of England is a government official. The king of England has designated duties to the government. Our king has no duties to the government. He is being paid for symbolism. But it's the only kingdom in the whole of Kenya.

The Luo community in Kenya occupies the Nyanza region. We talked about the Nyanza. That's Lake Victoria. They also live in big cities in Kenya, like Kisumu, Nairobi, and Mombasa. Their major city is Kisumu on Lake Victoria. The Kikuyu community in Kenya occupies the central and northern regions of Kenya. They have also moved into many areas in the Rift Valley region. Almost every city in Kenya has a Kikuyu community living there, has at least a Kikuyu person living there or working there. Kikuyus are very tenacious and quite industrial.

Caroline is of Wanga (her father) and Luo (her mother) descent. Two different tribes or communities. People often talk about people not marrying outside of their tribe or community. Regarding intermarriage, whether or not it was accepted is a bigger explanation than just yes, it was accepted, or no, it was not accepted. Luos did not know Kikuyus, and Kikuyus did not know Luos before colonial times. The Luos have been living in their area for over a thousand years, and the Kikuyus have been living in their area for over a thousand years. The Luyiah, which is my group, have been living in our area for over a thousand years. As well as many other groups. Unless you are near or not too far away from the nearest community outside of your own, you hardly know any other community way over there, miles and miles away. People did not travel that much; there was no means of traveling years and years ago. Because with the wilderness and the great distance between communities, you had to have a real good reason to go to the other communities even one hundred miles away or three hundred miles away. So only neighboring tribes, as you want to call it, or communities next to each other knew each other. With the creation of Kenya, which only happened at the end of the 1800s, we didn't know the rest of the Kenyans. We did not even regard them as our people. Now do you see that dichotomy that is cropping up here? Here, people who did not know each other, had never met, had never had interest in each other, and had never even heard of each other were now being told that they all belonged to Kenya—you belonged to this country. So given the disparity, it was hard to say when Luos and Kikuyus got married. When Kenya became independent, it was deliberate for Kenya's government to mix up students from one community with the other community. Like integration. So like with any other culture that is different from another culture, intermarriage is sometimes accepted and sometimes not accepted.

I will complete my portion of the narrative here by talking about the Bwibo women. Caroline is Bwibo. Bwibo are very influential in the community and are often very intimidating. Bwibo tend to gravitate toward their community and are protective and loyal. The males in the

Wanga kingdom who are of the ruling class are called Abashitsetse (singular for "the ruling clan") and Omushitsese (plural). Caroline is a Bwibo because I am a male from the ruling clan. I am Abashitsetse. It is not about Wanga. The blood of Bwibo flows from the father to the children. It is paternal. Some of the members of the Wanga kingdom were acquired by war. Remember, we expanded the kingdom by fighting alongside the Massai and the British, who were mercenaries. To the degree that they were invited to live among us and fight alongside us to overtake other clans and incorporate them into the Wanga community. The defeated clans became members of the Wanga either by force or by persuasion. We have twenty-two of them. They are not all Abashitsetse (of the ruling class), but they are all Wanga. Are the Bwibo born or created? First, if a daughter is born of a father who is a member of the ruling class, she is a Bwibo, but there is a thin line here. It is also a question of growing up and finding that your father, your brothers, and all the men in your family are behaving like warriors and rulers. You are a girl, and you acquire similar characteristics of being bossy, just because you grow up with everyone who looks like a boss. So they tend to be bossy, because the culture allows their men to be bossy toward others, and the young girls grow to display the same attitudes and characteristics of a boss. Caroline is Wanga and Bwibo, but Caroline is herself. That is it.

Ladies and gentlemen and everybody else, you have just experienced the source of my "I Can Do Anything" vibe, who, when I got promoted to vice president in corporate America, proclaimed, "You are a president."

# Bwibo [Bwee-bo]

Contrary to the words of twenty-first-century philosopher Beyoncé, I did not wake up like this. I begin with this premise to establish a foundational truth about Caroline. I am here, but I didn't start here. While that may seem obvious, as growth is built into the fiber of living, I've found that when people meet you where you are, they have difficulty allowing the story of where you've been or where you're going into their construct of "you." Social and internet media clips of my "best" moments and most profound quotes are not taken as "snapshots" in time. They are perceived instead as effortless expressions of who I've always been.

When my intentional journey of self-reflection and development began in earnest, I consumed every bit of self-help and self-development content I could get my hands on. The more I read, listened, and watched, the worse I felt, because it seemed to me that every philosophy worked, every story had a happy ending, every thought manifested the desired outcome, and every experience went exactly as planned because the journeys were from being a loser to being a winner. There seemed to be no room for failure, setbacks, or wrong turns, which I happen to have an abundance of. I resolved, during that time, that if I ever got to the point where my story mattered on a larger scale, I would always include the struggles, failures, impulsiveness, and self-sabotage that hindered and anchored my growth.

I guarantee you will find at least one point of connection in my story because we are not as different as you think we might be. The point of connection between us will assist you in fulfilling the unique purpose you offer to the world. *I'm Highly Percent Sure* that who you are is nonnegotiable. Put a pin in who you see now and let me tell you how I got here.

This is a human story.

I was born on an ordinary day that history would mark as extraordinary, the same day Daniel arap Moi seized the presidency of Kenya. But before we get too far down the road, let's rewind to precolonial Kenya through the lens of the Wanga kingdom. My father is of the Wanga people, and my mother is of the Luo people. I'm a cocktail of the Wanga and Luo peoples, a rich, complex, and vibrant heritage of the African tapestry. My parents, Dr. Pamela Wanga of the Luo tribe from Kisumu and Dr. Lucas Wanga of the Luyiah tribe from Kakamega. My parents are from different communities, and people from different communities do not often mix or marry each other.

A little context: In Kenya, your last name is more than just a name. It's an emblem, a signpost that announces your tribal roots. It's like wearing your heart on your sleeve, quite literally. Your tribal affiliation is in your name; you are born into it, and you can't change it. This means all the traditions, reputation, and socioeconomic existence of your tribe are automatically attributed to you. The only circumstance in which your tribal last name would change to a name outside your tribe is if you as a woman marry a man from outside your tribe. As children, we learned to appreciate the beauty of our heritage, understand the complexities of our multitribal family, and leverage it to thrive personally and professionally.

Before colonization, the Wanga was a thriving community. I'm sharing this because a lot of how I operate in the world is based on the tribal aspects of my family's history. What you will learn about my heritage will challenge the way the African continent and its people have been portrayed in the entertainment industry. While you can search the internet and libraries for all that has been written about the Wanga kingdom, my learnings were offered firsthand. My source was my dad, Dr. Lucas Wanga, whose knowledge spans a spectrum of what he studied, what his professional experiences are, and what his lived life continues to be.

For shits and giggles, there is a movie that was made in 1936 called *The Love Wanga*. My brothers bought me the movie poster one year for Christmas, and that's how we learned that "wanga" is also used as the description for a particular type of voodoo. On behalf of my ancestors, I'm coming to get my damn royalties, Hollywood!

While I have given you a lot of information on my dad's tribe, my mother's tribe is Luo. Let me just flex real quick on what the Luo people like to brag about related to their tribe. Most of them will brag about Barack Obama, the first Black president of the United States and a Nobel Peace Prize laureate, whose daddy was Luo. Then they would claim Academy Award winner Lupita Nyong'o, who was not only Luo but whose father was a Kenyan ambassador to Mexico, which is why her first name is of Spanish heritage. And if you were to ask my mama and her sisters who the third most famous Luo is, they would say me. Bless their exaggerating hearts. Just in case you don't believe me on how exaggerated my mama's narrative about me is, check out the next few paragraphs, where she tells the story of me. Ladies and gentlemen, I present to you Dr. Pamela Wanga and her perspective on the story of my birth. I'll see you all in a few. ENJOY!

My baby Caroline was born during the time I was at the tail end of completing my master's degree thesis at Kenyatta University, located on the outskirts of Kenya's capital city of Nairobi in Central Province. I dared to travel nearly three hundred miles so I could give birth close to Eregi College in western Kenya, where Caroline's father was teaching. A few days after my trip, baby Caroline was delivered at the private Victoria Hospital in Kisumu, managed by a team of Catholic sisters.

It was early Friday, January 13, 1978! A bouncing eight-pound, fifteen-and-a-half-ounce baby girl was placed on my chest. Yes, my first labor for such a healthy baby was long and excruciating, but holding this beautiful piece of human being with Afro hair and big, deeply penetrating eyes wiped away all the labor pain and replaced it with the pride and faith that this bundle of joy was special. Baby Caroline looked like she had come to this world with a planned purpose. She was ready for whatever . . . and I (we) have experienced it!

We named her Auma as her cultural first name, given because she was a posterior birth and because her late maternal great-grandmother's name was Auma. She inherited both the name, the legacy, and the position of birth—all in one baby. Cola, believe it or not, was a nickname she was given because I seriously craved (and got) Coca-Cola during the early parts of my pregnancy! Finally, Caroline became her baptismal name.

Caroline was a fearlessly superactive child. She was courageous, energetic, and inquisitive. Caroline attended the highly competitive Kenyatta University–sponsored elementary school. The school was located on campus and just about a seven-minute walk to our house; she always came home from school with a smile, bouncing her grades as if she wanted the paper to fly and inform the world of her excellent academic performance.

Caroline was in the third grade when she came home crying from school one afternoon. I asked her if she had gotten into a fight with a student or if something bad had happened to her. Caroline unzipped her backpack and pulled out her grade sheet. She had earned the top score overall in her finals. The teacher had changed the score to favor a male student (we'll call him Cran) whose father was a beginning lecturer at the university. Caroline commanded me to head to her school first thing in the morning to confront the teacher and make things right. She believed that her grade was lowered because of her gender. The student's father instigated that change because he was male, though in a lower position than me! I had my own issues regarding confronting the teacher. Caroline would be stigmatized even more because her proud mother, an educated "female" who had just returned with a PhD from a study abroad. I intervened, and Caroline's grade placed her in first position and the boy in second. Caroline portrayed an intense feeling against unequal practices. She demonstrated leadership concepts early in her childhood.

Caroline's adventures were atypical compared to babies born and traditionally raised in Kenya and Africa. Growing up, Caroline moved with us as a family everywhere we went; in Kenya, from Kenya to Edmonton, Alberta, Canada; back to Kenya, on to Minnesota, Texas College, and back to Minnesota. She is now an independent woman busy applying in-depth skills and traits while learning and developing to greater heights. We have lived in places that resembled palaces. We have dwelt close to slums, in shelters, with other families, and rotated through different sites and locations. The family has evolved together in good and not-so-good times. Strength of heart and soul and faith-led character have shielded every member of the family against all odds. To represent the sentiment that surrounded Cadence (Caroline's daughter) during the time of her college graduation. It was demonstrated that the Wanga family, through selflessness, support, and understanding, continued a legacy of love that fueled her postsecondary journey with the confidence to move forward with future stages of life.

In closing, I would reiterate one of Caroline's popular posts about a greeting of a nomadic tribe in Kenya: "Do you know where your children are?" which translates into "You are just as good as your children are; their failures, to some extent, make you a failure as well." This statement is a systems theory applied to family interactions; the whole is only as good as the sum of its parts. Caroline has pulled us along. We in turn have shared our pride and amazement across family, friends, and continents. She is an inspiration to all. We stand with and by her.

Did y'all enjoy my mama? Great, I'll pick it up from here!

My parents fundamentally believed that there was nothing I could not do. Therefore, I operated completely believing that I just needed to pick what I wanted to do and I would be able to do it. I was smart, creative, and open-minded when I pursued anything that I decided to. Being raised in Kenya meant I existed in a world where what I looked like was not a barrier to anything I wanted to do. The pastor, the prostitute, the policeman, and the president all looked like me, which meant my options were limitless in terms of what I looked like. The types of things that would have slowed me down were based on Kenya's society, such as things like gender, tribe, and socioeconomic status, to name a few.

I share this to counter the narrative that success stories like mine can only stem from a background marred by poverty, deficit, or tremendous struggle. At this point in my life, that simply was not my story. My childhood in Kenya and my parents' positions in the community of academia meant schoolwork was prioritized over everything else. That meant no chores. Housekeepers or other helpers gave me as much time as possible to focus on my education.

In 1987, my father left Kenya for the United States to complete his PhD at the University of Minnesota, and we followed nearly a year later in 1988. I was ten. My brother James was seven, and the twins, Victor and Vincent, were two.

When we came to America, what I experienced was contradictory to the mindset that I had previously existed in. It required a reeducation on how I would find success in this new environment. It was jarring, to say the least.

I found myself in the throes of Midwestern/American middle-school culture in a state called Minnesota. I was taller than all the girls and most of the boys. I was confronted with the barriers that my Blackness created. I had an accent, and the lunches my mom prepared for me, which I loved, smelled weird to my classmates. They used to remind me every day how much I didn't belong in their world.

To survive in this new and unfamiliar territory, I tried to protect myself by shrinking my intellect, adjusting my posture to look shorter than I was, and intentionally trying to lose my accent in an attempt to match what I saw around me aesthetically to try to blend in and not be seen.

Since I had been grounded in the reality of infinite possibility, my survival decisions dimmed my bright and burning fire of limitless aspiration to a flicker fueled by being average and unseen. This behavior subconsciously aligned with how the totality of Global Black has had to accommodate others to exist equally. We've had to diminish our strength, adjust our looks, minimize our creativity, and discount our economic contributions at the threat of death, ridicule, and violation of personal safety just to survive.

In the present day, I am considered a disrupter. Had I been as disruptive then as I am now, the pathology of how I experienced racism in America as a teenager would have been understood and would have included a plan to exist successfully. In the absence of that, I had to self-navigate the pathologies of oppression that were presented in a construct that recognized me as a "kind of Black" and depended on what my parents were unaware of, because they didn't know what it meant either. Hence, this season of my life resembles a head-on collision with the tumult of "breathing while Black" with no context as to why.

I tell people all the time: in hindsight, I can point to acts of racism toward me when I was growing up in Minnesota. Still, it remains an intellectual recounting, because when it happened, I didn't know it was racism. My parents knew about colonialism, but that is very different from racism, because the kingdom on the continent was thriving before it was colonized. So the colonial story is one of a continent of people conquering the British occupation of their homeland by fighting to get it back.

I would come home from school emotionally distraught and tell my parents, "I don't want to go back to school because the kids keep making fun of me." Their response was grounded in believing that whatever I experienced in school was within my control to change and make it better. Considering how conflicted I was by how my parents advised me to deal with what I was experiencing, I had no choice but to do the best I could to make it through each day, because even the teachers, staff, and counselors at school couldn't help.

Remember that place you tried to forget called junior high. Let me tell you why I tried to forget mine. So picture this . . . Roseville,

Minnesota, in the eighties. I'm pretty sure you don't know where that is. But for the sake of this story, then and now, very few people looked like me. Coming to a place like that, at ten years old, at the height of five feet, eight inches, with a tenor/alto voice and no sense of pop culture and fashion trends, made my daily existence the focus of every deprecating and demeaning word that junior high incites. Because of that, this moment was the beginning of me trying to get rid of anything that made me different, brought attention, and made me get picked on. Hence, the beginning of Caroline "trying" to make herself small and undiscoverable to survive.

From Roseville, Minnesota, to Minneapolis, Minnesota, I entered my sophomore year at Edison High School, expecting to survive the same way I did in junior high. However, the mix of classmates and cultures varied greatly from what I had previously experienced. I immediately noticed that more people looked like me, but what was more important was how much no group dominated the representation of my new classmates. In my last year at Roseville Middle School, I had been on the track team of Roseville High School, whose track program was highly ranked in the state. Because of that, I came to Edison High School more athletically skilled than I thought, which made transitioning into the sports ecosystem of the Minneapolis schools pretty seamless. Because I had been in a very competitive sports program before Edison, I quickly became one of the best-performing members of the Edison track team. That level of notoriety brought infinitely more positive attention from my classmates than I had ever experienced. I became more comfortable being seen and heard because I was popular and talented.

One of the unique things about the Minneapolis public school system, which included seven schools at that time, was that each school had a magnet program. Still, each school's magnet program was different. The magnet programs allowed high school–aged students to attend high schools that weren't necessarily in their immediate neighborhood, because they could select a magnet program that interested them. This is what I now understand to be the driver of the spectrum of diversity I saw in high school every day.

Edison's magnet programs included a childcare program with a full-time daycare center in the school, a cosmetology program with a fully functioning salon, an automotive program with a fully functioning mechanic shop in the school, and a culinary program with a fully functioning restaurant. Enrollment in these magnet programs equipped students with a trade skill they could use immediately upon graduation. But if you attended the school and were not a part of the magnet program, you could benefit from the services each program offered and delivered by your classmates. My friends worked on my car, they did my hair, they gave me eating options that weren't the cafeteria, and had I had a child at the time, they would have cared for that child on-site.

My clique was not only eclectic but also full of intelligent, skilled, smart-ass banter, and obnoxious and unwavering support of one another. Beyond my high performance in track and field, my coaches wanted me to play other sports to keep myself conditioned year-round. Because of my height, volleyball and basketball were added to my athletic agenda in the eleventh grade. My clique had my back when I played one sport. Nothing changed when I played three. Very rapidly, my athletic performance in three sports made me a popular girl, drawing superficial and insincere attention from people who hadn't cared who I was when I hadn't been popular. Having a clique that functioned like family was crucial for not falling back into trying to make myself small because of attention that didn't feel good.

Now I had a community within the school that allowed me to become comfortable in my skin; any negativity thrust at me didn't injure me because my clique protected and uplifted me. Whether there were vicious rumors or competitive jealousy or intentional threats, what the crew did was establish themselves as the wrath you would deal with if you tried to fuck with Caroline.

High school is the Wild West of adolescence. A chaotic mix of homework shoot-outs, popularity showdowns, sports face-offs, and imaginary fashion competitions. Now buckle up, 'cause we're about to take a roller coaster through three of the most positive and impactful years of my adolescence. Have y'all ever seen a porcupine shoot its quills? Well, I went to school with one. Let me introduce you to Ms. Porcupine. Although we never had a single class together, her favorite places to shoot her quills were the hallways in between classes, in the cafeteria, during volleyball and basketball practice, and whenever we saw each other in Northeast Minneapolis.

Our coexistence was often presented in the form of a rivalry between someone with earned athletic ability and someone with natural athletic ability. Because I was the latter, her perception of me was always one where she felt like I was a threat to her reputation, and therefore, we would engage in intellectual and psychological banter anytime we were around each other.

Ms. Porcupine had a knack for wielding words as weapons, always aiming for what she deemed my weak spots. "I'm going to Harvard, and you will never get in," she'd sneer during practice when we were paired up for drills and plays. Her words were laced with a toxic blend of malice and mean-girl energy. Her behavior came to a climax when I was selected to represent our school as the top female athlete for the prestigious statewide recognition known as the Athena Awards. The Porcupine assumed she was going to be selected and made sure that everybody in school knew how she felt about it our entire senior year. Plot twist—because the athletic director forced me to take senior pictures (I was not going to take senior pictures, but you needed one to submit for the award), I was made aware in advance that I had been selected as the 1995 Athena Award winner for Edison High School. I savored in silence that when she would find out that I had been selected, she would not only be disappointed but embarrassed about the narrative that she had created about winning the Athena Award all over the school.

So let me just give you the CliffsNotes of the story you just read. I was the tall girl, the one who basketball and volleyball coaches homed in on, pushing me into the ruthless world of high school sports, where every game was a struggle for survival. I was the towering figure who had never even touched a basketball or spiked a volleyball until the eleventh grade. But to the coaches, my height was a passport to glory. When I was thrust into the chaos, the court became a battlefield. I was a pawn in a game I had never asked to play. The battlefield extended beyond the court. High school was a whirlwind of relentless comparisons, a never-ending tug-of-war with Porcupine. On paper, we were mirror images, but in the reality of high school politics, we were worlds apart. Our rivalry became a bitter dance of resentment, with Porcupine hell-bent on asserting her superiority and me determined to rise above her petty games. In the high school circus, we were two rival acts. There were Porcupine's followers, and then there were my supporters. Our rivalry even extended to the race for student council presidency. My campaign slogan? "Vote for Diversity." She won, and, yeah, it hurt. To add insult to injury, the Porcupine and I ended up going to the same exact college. Spoiler alert: it wasn't Harvard.

# Shiiiiiiiiiiiiiiiiiiiiiiiiiiiit

Spoiler Alert: An *H* school did end up being the post–high school destination for Porcupine and me, but that *H* was Hamline University. Now, there are several other *H* words that I could offer here, but y'all got a book to read. Catch me outside, guess your *H* word, and I'll let you know if you're right.

Another *H* is "heptathlete," like an Olympic-level heptathlete, like a Jackie Joyner-Kersee–level heptathlete. The heptathlon is seven events over a few days that are dominated by those in track and field who are competitive in several events in a predetermined sequence. I was that, and therefore, the Olympics as a heptathlete was my deepest aspiration. There was an eighth event that I had neither trained for nor predicted. I discovered it because my best friend and I would frequently go to a clinic and pee on a stick because she always thought she was pregnant. We got so used to going and getting negative pregnancy results that we stopped being scared that she would test positive for being pregnant. I just knew that I was never going to be the pregnant one. I was going because I was her best friend, until one day, the nurse came out and pointed at me, and I quickly responded, "I'm just here to support her." Then the nurse asked, "Is your name Caroline?" I responded, "Yes," and then she said, "You're pregnant." I literally froze and was probably in shock. My best friend was looking at me, trying to figure out how to help me, and all I could think about was losing my track scholarship, because now I had a motherfucking eighth event. It didn't have shit to do with track, it didn't have shit to do with the Olympics except for the fact that I was finally going to be the Kenyan my track coach always wished I had been, but this marathon was going to be MOTHERHOOD.

For the record, none of the biological indicators that you are pregnant happened to me. I had no missed periods, no nausea, no weight gain, etc. After the shock of the visit to the clinic, the next thing I remember is going to a pay phone to call the guy I was pretty sure I was pregnant by. He was the only guy I was seeing. We hadn't known each other very long. I was surprised that he was elated about the news of my being pregnant.

In the next couple of weeks, as I processed the fact that I was pregnant, I distinctly remember the way I informed my mom of my pregnancy. My mom and I were in a fight about something stupid. I don't even remember what it was about. I think it was about the dishes.

"Caroline, when are you going to do the dishes? I've been asking for a while."

As I rolled my eyes, I responded, "Mom. I'll get to it when I get to it."

"You will get to it now, not when you want to."

With the very special seasoning that teenagers put on everything they say, I yelled, "That's why I'm pregnant!" Then I went to my room and slammed the door shut.

As I continued to process my pregnancy, I began to feel the emotional weight of my family's reputation and my future now that I was going to be a mother at seventeen years old. I would have given anything to unsee the disappointment that washed over my mother's face when I told her. I said to my mom, "I know everybody thinks I'm going to fail. I'm going to prove that I am not a failure." From that moment on, it was all about me and my baby.

I didn't have health insurance at the time, so I got all my prenatal care at a sliding-fee clinic in Minneapolis. My pregnancy journey had only the bare minimum preventative care necessary when you are pregnant. It is part of why I only had one ultrasound to check on the health of the baby and was not able to get any additional ultrasounds to know my baby's gender or any other preferential information people want to know about their baby.

None of the traditional celebratory routines were a part of my journey. There's rumored to be only one picture of me while I was pregnant. I didn't consciously try to avoid it, but I didn't celebrate it. There was no maternity shoot. There was no looking at my belly growing. There was no baby shower. There was nothing commemorative. Everybody was disappointed and embarrassed and therefore seemed to feel more comfortable ignoring my presence than celebrating the life I was bringing into the world. Everybody around me was heartbroken, and I felt that every day.

I didn't read any books about pregnancy. The only book I looked at was a book to try to pick a name. My baby used to kick to a beat in my stomach. There didn't have to be music playing, but whatever it was, the beat was consistent. So when I was trying to decide what to name my baby and stumbled upon a musical term that intuitively seemed to make sense based on how my baby behaved in my stomach, I chose that name for my baby. It was one of the first affirming decisions I made when I decided to name my baby Cadence.

My mother was there during my pregnancy. We interacted because I was still living at home, but Mom and I didn't really talk about it. My father was another story. He couldn't speak to me, which was devastating for this daddy's girl. My cousins weren't allowed to talk to me. It was like my being pregnant was contagious. It wasn't comfortable at home, and everybody I encountered seemed to be grieving. At that point, everything became about proving everyone wrong. I was determined to be a great mom, finish college, and be what I knew I could be. I wasn't going to give anyone permission to renegotiate my potential.

Once I decided to keep Cadence, I knew it meant dropping out of college. So I left college my first semester, and Porcupine had all kinds of things to say, but what was now more important in my life was caring for my child rather than paying attention to the rumors that Porcupine was spreading. Later on in life, I would pay attention to whether I was doing better than her, but how she felt about me becoming a teenage mother faded more and more as I got older.

I lived at home during my pregnancy, and I was determined not to be a statistic, and that started with getting a job. I returned to the only places I knew. Throughout my pregnancy, I continued the job I started in high school at the Mall of America movie theater. I just kept my head down, focused on working to support my daughter. It was beneficial to work at the movie theater because most of the time, my belly was behind a counter. A lot of people didn't even know I was pregnant until I was about six or seven months along. The only reason people at work found out was because I asked for a new shirt size. I never needed maternity clothes because I have a long torso, and the way she sat in my stomach, she didn't cause my stomach to protrude out, so I wore a lot of jogging suits. Even with the people who knew I was pregnant, there wasn't a lot of chatter, because I didn't look pregnant.

I worked in the movie theater up until the day before I gave birth. I vividly remember the morning of the day Cadence was born. My water broke when I went to pee, so I hadn't known it had broken. I didn't realize I was in labor that day; it was very similar to the way I found out I was pregnant. No precursors or warnings. I wasn't getting all this *What to Expect When You're Expecting* education. I was just pregnant. I was seventeen. I had been training to be an Olympic heptathlete. I was the epitome of health; I didn't walk around worried about having her and what that would be like. I was like, *She'll come when she comes.*

That morning, I told my mom my stomach hurt. She asked if my water had broken, and I said no, because I really hadn't known. She thought I was having Braxton-Hicks contractions, so I went back to sleep. About thirty minutes later, I felt a different kind of pain. I called out to my mother. She monitored me, and then she realized they were the real contractions, and she took me to the hospital. After a few hours of labor, Cadence was born.

There was a calm and comfort that came after Cadence was born. She was a reconciliatory trigger within my family. My brothers thought the whole thing was cool. After Cadence was born, they loved and doted on her and treated her like a little sister. My parents were instantly in love with her too.

While I was grateful to have given birth to a healthy baby girl, I still had some unresolved feelings about college and the pressure to finish my bachelor's degree. However, it was more important to find a job that would support all the new needs that came with being a mother.

During high school, I had been a camp counselor during the summers. So I went back to that same organization to see if they still had any full-time positions available. They hired me full-time to run after-school programs for kids in the Twin Cities, which was the beginning of my work in the nonprofit world. While I found quite a bit of success during my seven years in the nonprofit sector, there came a point in which not having a degree was impacting my ability to earn more income. When people would tell me that my lack of a degree was impacting my upward mobility, I would often respond by informing them that I would not be any smarter if I went to school, so why not just give me the job now? Even though they could have chosen to override the degree requirements for the next job I wanted to have, they chose not to because they did not want to upset the internal organizational processes. I tried numerous options to pursue my bachelor's while working full-time, but none accommodated everything I needed to further my education as a single parent.

In addition to working full-time, I volunteered at the Minneapolis chapter of the NAACP. While there, I received an email about an HBCU (Texas College) in Tyler, Texas, that had set aside funding to start a program to help single parents finish their degrees. It was perfect for my situation: my child could live with me in my dorm, I would have transportation to and from school, and there were a Boys & Girls Club for after school and a daycare. My child would be able to eat in the cafeteria with me; the college would also assist

31

with book costs and connect me with scholarship opportunities. The program had the essential things I needed to further my educational journey as a single parent.

I visited Texas College in October and left Minnesota for Texas the following January. I told my close friend Lauretta about the program for single parents. She was a single parent working at a nonprofit and was just about ready to move up as well. I was Texas-bound by January, but Lauretta needed more time to flip the switch. She made the move to Tyler a few semesters later.

There was so much pressure from everyone and everywhere for me to go back to school and so much emphasis on getting that degree that it became as much about shutting everyone up as it was about furthering the things I wanted to do. I didn't know anyone in Texas. I didn't know anyone on campus. It was more about how I needed to get this degree thing out of the way, because it was getting in the way of my taking care of my daughter.

A little over a year after Cadence and I moved to Tyler, my mom, out of nowhere, came to Tyler and eventually ended up as a professor in the Education Department at Texas College. None of us understood why, so we just figured she needed a change, and Cadence and I became the story that people would accept about why she moved. By the time my mother moved to Tyler, my brother Victor was already in Tyler with me after a falling-out with my dad. A little bit after my mother arrived, my brother Vincent decided to move to Tyler. He didn't have a grand plan or a detailed road map for his life. He just needed a place to crash while he figured shit out. He was one of those kids who choose to take a gap year to think about what they want to do after graduation. His move to Tyler was more of a pit stop. Soon after Vincent arrived in Tyler, my brother Victor chose a completely different direction. He enlisted in the Marines and left Texas. During those years in Texas, Vincent, my mom, Cadence, and I got pretty tight, supporting one another in all of our various pursuits. Everybody loved my mom. Her students thought she was everything. Everybody knew she was my mom, so when I was crowned homecoming queen of Texas College in 2005, my mom was right there alongside Ms. Loretta X. Dewberry, who was responsible for all logistics tied to being the campus queen and planning my coronation. Between my mom and Ms. Dewberry, everything was a little extra, which was on full display when my mom dressed Cadence for my coronation like it was a royal wedding.

When Lauretta arrived, we were practically joined at the hip. People at school were fascinated by the fact that we were from Minnesota; they were fascinated with our height too. From time to time, they would come to us and verify that we were really from Minnesota and ask us if all the Black people in Minnesota were tall. Lauretta and I had been best friends since our children had been toddlers. What people saw were two women who behaved as sisters and two kids who behaved as siblings. We were tight, and always together. Folks knew us as the two Black girls from Minnesota. Having Lauretta there was motivating in every way. Besides being support systems for each other, we were equals intellectually, and we had so much in common. We usually had the highest grades in any class we had together. The one thing she didn't do was sports, but Lauretta could and still can sing her ass off. Back in Minnesota, when I befriended Lauretta, she invited me to the church that she attended, and I eventually became a member of her church. That church family is now our shared family, even to this day. Lauretta was the buzz of Texas College because of her soulful voice, and she became the heart of the college choir while I was the Student Government Association president. She was a political science major to my business major. I selected business because it was the most flexible, and she selected political science because she wanted to make an impact in the world. She ultimately decided to further her education and get a graduate degree. So she left Tyler and headed to Alabama A&M, focusing on urban planning and housing. Lauretta still lives in Huntsville, Alabama, doing the work she loves.

I started at Texas College at the age of twenty-five, but without the fervor and excitement that most people have when they start college. I used my frustration over getting a degree that I did not think I needed to get promoted to fuel my turning four years of school into two and a half years. Twenty-one credits a semester, including in January and the summer. I graduated with a degree in business administration. After graduating, I thought, *Well, I'm in Texas now, and I'm not going back to the cold weather back in Minnesota. I'm going to figure out what job to do here in Texas.*

# I Guess I Do Like People

I really liked Texas, and the idea of living in Dallas was appealing to me because it was warm and metropolitan, which was very different from living in Tyler. Finishing my degree in two and a half years meant I was a December graduate, so my internship ended up being the summer before my last semester. I was a business major because it was the most flexible thing I could do and still advance in my career. I was able to secure a summer internship but was not excited about it because my daughter was not going to be able to go with me. I would have to give my daughter to my mom or somebody for the summer. She was in Tyler with me, and I wanted to keep her with me. So I was secretly looking for an internship that would allow her to be with me for the summer.

A representative from the Target Distribution Center came on campus for a career fair because his wife was the secretary to the president of Texas College. I knew Target, and I was like, "What are y'all doing here?" He talked about what was happening at their distribution center, which was about twelve miles from my college. All I wanted to know was how much they were paying, because taking this internship meant my daughter could stay with me for the summer. Once they told me the hourly rate was more than what the other internship was paying, that fact finalized my decision to take the Target opportunity. When my internship with Target ended, I was grateful, but I didn't expect anything more to come from it. Unbeknownst to me, they had considered my class schedule, and they offered me a leadership position starting immediately, working Tuesday through Friday nights while finishing my degree.

Mark Irvin, who, at the time of this writing, was the chief supply chain officer for Best Buy, was a really important advocate for me when he was at Target. He was one of the very few Black senior leaders that I saw, and I remember going to his office and accepting the job, even though I was unsure of what I wanted to do at Target long-term.

While in Mark's office, I told him why I took the job but also confessed that I still needed to figure out what I wanted to be at Target. He started laughing and said, "I know. It's okay. I just don't want you to miss out on the opportunity." In my head, I was still thinking, *What the hell do I know about moving boxes from point A to point B?* The conversation I had with Mark that day was what led to me to create my first career map. He told me to stop trying to figure out what I wanted to be inside of the organization and instead define some experiences I wanted to have. He said, "Once you get that figured out, it will inform you what you want to be and if you still want to be here." He was 100 percent correct, so I created a career map, and that exercise guided the first five years of my Target career.

My first career map was focused on experiences I wanted to have to help me determine what I wanted to be at Target. This is an example of what it looked like.

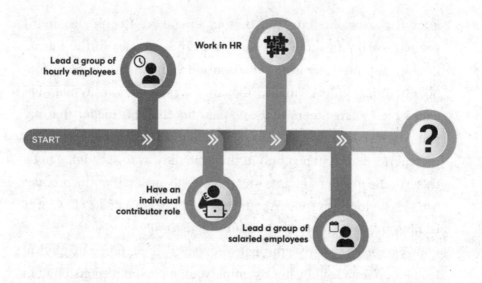

Each experience was defined as a goal, not a role. Each goal listed three things that I wanted to get from the experience. Once those were achieved, it was time for me to move on to the next experience. Before I left an experience, I had to categorize what I learned as either a strategic "yes," which meant it had the potential to be something I would want to do long-term, or a strategic "no," which meant it was not something I would want to do long-term. Part of how this map guided my first five years while working at the distribution center in Tyler was that I evangelized it to my bosses, peers, HR, and senior leaders who would visit from Target headquarters. My request of them was to be on the lookout for existing and upcoming roles they thought would fit my experience goals and my career map's intent.

Why did I choose these experiences? Target is a retail business. Hourly employees comprise almost 80 percent of the employee workforce at stores and distribution centers nationally, which made leading large groups of hourly employees a critical experience on my map. It was essential to have that experience so I could decide if I wanted to stay in retail and do those types of roles in the future. Luckily, my first role in the distribution center that shipped products to Target stores satisfied that first experience on my map because I led a large team that was paid hourly. This meant that my primary responsibility was ensuring that the team met specific KPIs (key performance indicators) in the time they were scheduled to be there in the most productive way possible to ensure that the product arrived at stores on time. Another experience I needed to have was leading salaried employees, because it naturally becomes a part of your career as you rise through the ranks. It's a different kind of leadership from leading hourly employees; my main responsibility in this role was to ensure that I was providing the right guidance within the correct time for people who reported to me but functioned autonomously. Under duress, I listed an experience in human resources because people thought I would be successful in HR. I had no intention of fulfilling it. I also listed an experience of being an individual contributor (meaning no direct reports). This was important because it was an experience where I was not leading a team, and I had not yet decided if I wanted to lead teams or not.

As I accomplished the goals of my first experience (leading a group of hourly employees), I shared my career map with a group of leaders from headquarters, and they connected me with an individual contributor role. The role I was offered (operations group leader) was in the distribution planning and engineering team at headquarters. (Yes, I ended up back in Minneapolis.) This role was focused on building perishable food distribution centers. Target wanted to expand its presence as a grocery business by growing its Super Target strategy. This was a perfect example of a job that nobody knew was coming, in a department that I would have never selected for myself, in a location I had sworn not to return to. This further reinforced the value of evangelizing my map to as many people as possible.

I learned a lot in this job, but I never thought I would know as much about bananas and turkeys as I currently do, so now I'm going to force you to know about turkeys and bananas too. Bananas are the divas of the produce industry. A grocery store isn't legit if they don't have bananas! They are hella high-maintenance and hella low price and expensive as hell to produce. I know that doesn't make sense, but it's true. These jokers have rooms especially for them, special blankets, and a special spectrum of colors that determine where they are to be stored, shipped, stocked, and sold. Now turkeys! It is not my fault if you don't like turkeys after what I'm about to tell you. Have you ever noticed that turkeys never go on sale? Well, let me tell you why. As long as they are kept at the right temperature, turkeys can be restored and resold for up to seven years. So that Thanksgiving turkey you had in 2023 could be from as far back as 2016. You're welcome!

My role as operations group leader was tied to a project timeline; therefore, I was constantly thinking about what I wanted to do once the project ended. I went back to my career map, and there were only two experiences left: to lead salaried people and to have a role in HR. Because I was at headquarters, I was somewhat open to seeing what HR opportunities existed at headquarters versus in the field. I decided to test the waters and prove wrong the people who said they thought I would be good in HR. And just like I thought, I interviewed for five HR roles and got turned down for all of them. So I was ready to go back to distribution.

Naturally, I started looking at HR roles that supported the distribution function I was already in because my business acumen could potentially be a valuable asset. In talking with distribution HR, I was told that to transition into that department, I would have to take a demotion and go back out into the field, and neither one of those options—less money and moving—would work for me. I did not close the door on HR opportunities at headquarters after talking with distribution HR. Instead, I looked for HR roles that were not generalist roles to see if I was a good fit for other parts of HR. That search led to interviews in the following HR business areas: recruiting, pay and benefits, organizational effectiveness, and HR operations. Despite glowing reviews after every interview, none of those interviews resulted in my being offered a job. Which further affirmed for me that HR was not a good fit for me. Unbeknownst to me, HR hadn't given up on me like I had given up on HR. Nevertheless, I turned my sights toward roles within distribution, fully aware of the ticking clock on my current role. My boss, who was frustrated about HR's continued activities that produced no positive results, gave me his full support. He expressed that sentiment to HR. "Don't put her through another interview if you aren't going to hire her. It's not fair," he told them.

I was opening our new distribution center in Cedar Falls, Iowa, when my boss came to me and said, "There's one more HR interview." And I was like, "Absolutely not. I'm done. HR has seen me inside and out. If they wanted me, they would have made me an offer. I'm done being paraded around as the distribution girl trying to get into HR." He understood my frustration because he was just as annoyed. He said, "If you go to this interview and they don't give you the job, I'll never ask you to interview for HR again." I agreed, not because I was hopeful but because I was annoyed. I thought, *Fine. If that's what it takes to end this charade, let's do it.*

This now meant that I had to leave Cedar Falls, Iowa, and get to

Minneapolis the next morning. In any other circumstance, this would not be enough time to prepare for an interview, but because I had no intention of getting the job, I didn't care. I cared so little about whether I would get the job that when I interviewed, I didn't even ask about the timeline for informing people once they chose the person for the job. So imagine my surprise when, by the time I returned to Cedar Falls on the afternoon of my interview, my boss found me and told me to expect a call from HR that day. Unexpectedly, the call I got was to offer me an HR generalist role supporting the property development business. I took the position, and now that position fulfilled the third experience on my career map.

As I started my role in HR as an HR business partner, I understood why people thought I would be a good fit for HR. I have a natural gift for influencing people, and what I learned was that HR is more about the "human" part of its name than the "resources" part of its name. My tenure as an HR generalist (which is usually the HR person at any job you have previously held) started in property development, then business intelligence, followed by Target.com/multichannel, which was also the role that included managing salaried people—the fourth experience left on my career map.

The skills and experiences I gained from these projects were invaluable, opening doors to opportunities that most didn't know existed. The challenges and uncertainties of these projects weren't daunting because I had become so accustomed to functioning while building. I became the person to call when an enterprise project needed someone who could quickly assimilate into an undefined landscape and drive it forward. Whether it was dot-com or business intelligence, my involvement was constant. There was a sense of "We need Caroline on this," whether it was building a job framework or pioneering a new business strategy. Without even realizing it, I was developing an "accidental skill" that propelled my career forward, allowing me to lead various projects and initiatives.

Over my five years in HR, I had the opportunity to be at the heart of Target's most important business strategies. I was now in the fourth experience on my career map, which was intended to tell me what I wanted to do within Target from a career perspective. One afternoon, I was complaining about the Black Employee Resource Group as a Black employee at Target. The person I was complaining to happened to work in the Office of Diversity and Inclusion (D&I). As part of our debate, he challenged me to fix what I thought was broken by pushing me to apply to lead the Black Employee Resource Group. The deadline to apply was at the end of that day that I was arguing with him. So being the stubborn person that I am, I applied that day and was subsequently selected to lead the Black Employee Resource Group. When I started in the employee resource group (ERG) role, which was just an added captainship to my actual job that was still in HR, I was further exposed to the Office of Diversity and Inclusion, because the Office of D&I manages all the employee resource groups in the company. The Office of D&I reminded me of the community work that I loved when I was working in the nonprofit arena. Therefore, I set my sights on moving into the Office of D&I because it was the closest to a soul that I thought I would find in corporate. The ERG role became an unplanned fifth experience on my first career map, while I was in my HR role.

It was the summer of 2012, and I started to develop a plan to get from my current role to the Office of D&I. This became my second career map. As an HR generalist, I had the flexibility to support several different businesses; therefore, I organized my map by what

HR roles I wanted that aligned with the business functions that worked with the Office of D&I. Additionally, I promoted myself every two years (on the map) and determined that I wanted to be the vice president of diversity and inclusion by July 2018, and I was going to give Target the right of first refusal. Similar to my first map, I defined the experiences and the goal I wanted each experience to meet. I shared the map with my boss, my HR partner, and the person who was currently the VP of D&I. Similar to how people viewed my first career map, everyone I shared my second career map with appreciated the clarity, and although no one told me, "Yes, you will be the VP of D&I," no one told me no either. That was good enough for me.

It was the end of 2013, and an opportunity presented itself for me to manage the acquisition of a new company that Target had its sights set on acquiring. I expected a call from my boss to give me all of the details of the position, including a relocation to California. As I anticipated, my boss got in touch with me and briefed me on everything related to the California position. In addition, she provided me with supplementary information about an upcoming vacancy on the D&I team, specifically for the role of vice president of D&I. After discussing it, the HR leadership team expressed their complete support for me to take on the role of VP of D&I. My boss informed me I had to choose between the two options, as it would not be possible to do both. If I were to accept the D&I job, it would be a promotion, which would make it impossible for me to return to the California job since it would be a lower rank. The D&I role would no longer be an option for me if I accepted the position in California, because they couldn't wait for me to fill it. Although the offer to take the role of VP of D&I came five years earlier than I had planned on my career map, accepting it just felt right. It was what

I'd asked for, and I knew that if I passed on it this time around, the opportunity wasn't gonna come again. So in February 2014, I accepted the position of vice president of diversity and inclusion at Target.

My first career map took ten years to achieve; I expected my second map to take six years based on what I had laid out. Sharing my map with key stakeholders had always been a key part of the process, but what it had also done was expose me to information about roles that I would not have known about otherwise. The role that brought me to headquarters to work in the food business was never posted and was part of a project that few people knew about. I got that role within a year of sharing my career map. Sharing my second map with key stakeholders created an opportunity to fill a role that was business-critical and could not sit vacant; therefore, a succession plan for an incumbent had to be developed. Although I expected my second map to place me in D&I in six years, when I shared my map, it manifested the D&I role on my career map in eighteen months, with unanimous support from senior leadership. My affinity for the career map process is tied to the fact that every career map I have created has manifested the exact right positions because of how and when I made it visible and to whom. It proves that while your career is impacted by the decisions of others, you are equipped to strategically conduct and participate in how it comes to life. The more clarity you give to those you want to support you, the easier it is to get the support you want.

# Her Name Is Cadence

Parallel to my career journey, another story was unfolding—the story of motherhood, of being Cadence's mom. Cadence and I stayed in Tyler, Texas, for five years before moving back to Minnesota. When I left Minnesota for Tyler, Texas, Cadence was just seven years old. When we returned to Minnesota in 2009, Cadence was a preteen, and my decisions revolved around her. It was a delicate dance of motherhood during a critical stage of Cadence's life, junior high demanding nurturing, patience, and a lot of love. It was important to have a supportive spiritual community and the right educational environment for her. We joined the same church that we attended before leaving for Tyler, Texas. I enrolled her in the same school she had attended before we had left. We returned to Minnesota in October, smack in the middle of the school year. It didn't make sense to uproot her again, so she returned to her old school's familiar environment. I wasn't just coming back to Minnesota with a well-paying job at Target; I was coming back with means, with the ability to choose. But even with the financial freedom, my decisions were guided by Cadence's needs and interests.

Only my dad and brother James were still in Minnesota. Victor had moved to Japan as a part of his career in the Marines Corps. My mom was still in Tyler, and a year after I left Tyler, she took a role leading the Teacher Education Department at the Southern University at New Orleans (SUNO) and moved to New Orleans.

For the first nine months after Cadence and I got back to Minnesota, we lived in Target corporate housing, which was cool, especially since everything felt so different now. Having been a resident of Minnesota for over two decades prior, I would have never chosen to live in downtown Minneapolis. Now that we were living in downtown Minneapolis, our routines were different from before; Cadence's school pickup and drop-off, grocery shopping, time with friends for both me and Cadence, my commute to work, as well as having to leave downtown to do extracurricular activities. Those nine months in downtown Minneapolis allowed me to make intentional decisions as to where and how Cadence and I wanted to live in this phase of our time in Minneapolis. This was an opportunity to upgrade how we would live. I don't mean that in the sense that something was broken. I mean it was about rebuilding, because almost everything was new. It was still familiar in terms of the location; not much had changed in that regard. But my tribe, my peeps, my family, even folks I knew casually were all either gone or not around. I knew I needed an anchor, something I could hang my heart on so I wouldn't find myself making rash decisions. For me, that meant getting back to my previous church home, Kwanzaa Community Church (Liberty Community Church). I was faithful to my commitment to the church. Even when I didn't feel like going, I got my butt up and went anyway. For five or six years, I was all in. I volunteered and led ministries and commit-tees. It was sort of a full-circle moment, because my nonprofit ex-perience once again came into play. It felt really important as much for me as for Cadence as well. I wanted her to have the feeling of belonging, consistency, and a spiritual foundation.

The story of how Cadence ended up in a STEM school is one of those moments in my parenting journey that I'm genuinely proud of. There are not a lot of moments that I talk about in that way. Cadence came home one day and said she wanted to go to a math school. I was like, "What on earth is a math school?" But that led me to discover the STEM program. Cadence was accepted into the STEM program and started playing on the volleyball team at that school.

Cadence thrived in that program, and as a parent, I believe that taking the time to listen to Cadence at that moment and actually look for a solution that matched what she was trying to say was crucial. Cadence was a great student. She wasn't frustrated. She was decisive. She said that math was her favorite subject and wanted to go to a school where she could do math all day. Listening to her, finding a program that matched, and then seeing how much that decision helped her thrive for the rest of her academic career were moments I'm really proud of. Because Cadence was clear about what she wanted made a big difference. I could have just put her in more math classes in her school. But I took it as "Here's what Cadence needs." She adored that program. I don't know if Cadence would have found the same joy in attending a regular school that didn't have that STEM twist. I don't think she would have done poorly, but she got excited about being in that program rather than just doing well in school. It was a different kind of excitement and joy, and it came with many inconveniences, but it was more than worth it.

The dynamic between my job at Target and Cadence was a juggling act. I was on the move a lot, creating a network of folks who could step in when I had to jet off for work. Because Cadence wasn't driving yet, she couldn't get herself from point A to point B. Sometimes I'd be gone for a week. Sometimes I would be away for much longer. It was frequent and often unpredictable. I could be off to one of four locations, considering we were building four distribution centers simultaneously.

I had to get creative, roping in people who could help when I had to travel for work. My brother James and his girlfriend, Chantel, were usually my first choice. They had a niece, Naomi, about the same age as Cadence. They picked up Cadence when they had Naomi, and the girls played together. If James and Chantel weren't available, I had a distant cousin I could ask, or I'd turn to my church family. Sometimes I'd lean on who I was dating if I needed someone to watch Cadence. Cadence never experienced separation anxiety because from the moment she was born, she was used to being around my family all the time. However, it did present different challenges when she started junior high school. It wasn't odd in terms of routine, but there were times when I'd get called at the last minute and have to fly out on short notice. I'd feel guilty. There were times when I couldn't find anyone, and I just had to bring Cadence with me. That wasn't the best decision, but I did it anyway. The guilt was more about the person I asked to help me out as opposed to guilt about Cadence, because this would be rushed: "Okay, pack now, you're going to stay at Auntie's house."

Cadence is a gracious child. She's pretty accommodating. She's an only child, so relationships and friendships are important to her because they are like siblings to her. What became more of an issue for Cadence was when she started playing sports. Because then it wasn't that there weren't people who could help me get her there. It was that I wasn't there. That was really when the issues came about—when her sports schedule started to create a place where I couldn't always be present. I think that was when it became problematic for her. I was astute enough to communicate to her that I couldn't be like the other volleyball moms. I told her I had to go to work, so I wouldn't be able to decorate her locker, host her whole team at our home for spaghetti dinner, or work the concession stand, because it was just me. I didn't have anybody to split those duties with. It was either the mom or the dad of the other players who could switch off their duties and share the responsibilities. There was this checklist of things the parents had to do for their kids to be in the program. I remember having to say to her, "I know this will feel weird, but I'm not like Madison's mom and dad." I used to sometimes split the duties with my brothers. But by that time, everybody had moved away from Minnesota. I explained that part to her because I knew what my coming in as a single parent into that kind of infrastructure would create for her. I tried to explain it to Cadence, but it didn't mean it made her feel better. You can only understand what you can understand at eleven, twelve, and thirteen.

I felt guilty, but the guilt started way before her junior high school days. It began when I had a kid at seventeen, so it had taken up permanent residency. It was always present. That would never go away. I think for me, my logic was to make sure she didn't believe that my inability to operate like those other parents meant I didn't support her.

As you can imagine, the other parents—aside from the Black woman who had the other Black daughter on the team—didn't make Cadence feel any better about it. In fact, what they would give her was pity. "Oh, your mom's not here again. Do you want to come over to our house?" It was unnecessary. They were just as much a part of the problem. I shared my feelings and concerns with Cadence, so at least she had my perspective to lean into when the conversation was happening around her. I would say to her, "Don't let what other people say to you about my presence or lack thereof cause you to think that I care about you differently." I was honest and more, like this was just a fact of our lives, because I didn't want her to hold out for a moment when it would change. It wasn't going to. Even if I had gotten married and whatever that would have been like, I don't think there would have been that much of a change that she would have realized in that junior high time frame around me being more present.

It was rough for us both. When I did make it to Cadence's games or events at school, other parents would throw shade at me. I would be physically present, and they'd still be like, "Oh, look who decided to join us." They would say dumb shit like that; most of them were white, so there was that part. It wasn't even that they were throwing it just at Cadence and then would shut it down with me; they would do it to me too. They hated me, because when they would shoot those comments at me, I would look at them and be like, "Look, who gets to stay home all day and think about volleyball?" I would tell them to shut up. That's how I would come back at them. I would be like, "Guess what I wasn't doing at home last night? Sleeping! You slept last night. I didn't. And I'm here." They would claim to be joking. "We were just kidding. Sorry." Then I'd get all that passive-aggressive white-guilt shit. I don't have time to help you with all that. Eventually, they stopped saying that stuff because I scared them. For me, my daughter needed to see me stand up to them when I was able to be there, because I know they were saying that shit when I wasn't around, and that was my problem with it all. That is what would piss me off. We could have this conversation with one another as adults; we should not be having this type of conversation in the presence of our children. I honored that, and they didn't. This is the type of cowardly behavior I would constantly call out.

There was one set of parents that I actually enjoyed and befriended—the parents of the only other Black girl on the volleyball team. Part of what came with that friendship was trust in leaving Cadence in their care when I needed to, and I appreciated them for that. This mother understood why it was important to speak up on Cadence's behalf when other parents would say inappropriate things in front of Cadence when I wasn't present. Their home was the only home I would let Cadence go to. I'd break my back to get her there because they understood and would step in appropriately. Unfortunately, since Cadence and her Black teammate were the only two Black girls on the team, they were often pitted against each other, but they became friends anyway. So anytime they were doing a team thing and I couldn't make it, I would give her friend's mom the money and ask her to bring Cadence with her. She kind of became Cadence's pseudo-mom when I couldn't be there.

If I can offer any advice to parents and caregivers: First, I believe that accountability in this stage of an adolescent's life is on the adults, not the kid. The kid is not at a place of maturity to activate a different existence. Everybody should get a prize for surviving junior high and its gauntlet of nonsense. Mitigating the trauma that junior high can create is on the adults. It is imperative to really understand what your child enjoys and, during that time, overly immerse them in the thing that they're either good at or they really enjoy. This gives them an outlet to feel valued and seen. I remember when I joined track and field and started to become good at that in high school. Whether it was real or not, suddenly, I was "Miss Popular" because I was good at track, which meant all that other bullshit didn't have the same impact. I had all these superficial friends who were friends with me because I was a good athlete. But I didn't care whether they were real or not. I just cared that people thought of me and were like, "That's Caroline; she's dope because of her athletics." It was very much the same with Cadence being in volleyball; she was a star on the court, so no matter what else she was experiencing, the fact that she was a star player was the counterbalance. People loved her and she was popular because she was great at volleyball.

Second, try to be clear and learn what makes your child different from the other kids in junior high. Monitor how those things bring forth interactions and activate protection, because adolescence and junior high are difficult for most people. I think a lot of parents are just like, "It's just junior high. It won't always be this way." Parents coach through their experiences, and kids can't articulate everything they need in junior high. The things that are different become the places of pain, because that's what kids pick on. Mine was my height. I was five-foot-eight at the age of eleven. Mine was my deep voice. Mine was the darkness of my skin, the texture of my hair, and the smell of my lunch. Those were the things that made me different from the other kids, which meant they were the things kids would pick on me about. Every kid has those things. It could be that they have braces. It could be that they are overweight. The important part is to know what makes your kid different from the other kids, because that's where the kids are going to come for them. Activate protection in the form of processing the events of the day every night. Ask questions even if they don't want to engage. It is almost as important to know that you are engaged as it is for them to reciprocate. It doesn't mean they can change what will happen the next day, but it allows you to intercept the way that those messages are being received and played forward by the kid so that they don't take as strong of a root. It does become their junior high experience. You cannot stop the experience, because teenagers are assholes. You can intercept messages daily based on the curated set of pain your child is experiencing and prevent it from taking root. Let it be a bad day, not a bad life. And if you do that regularly, but you start to see it manifest beyond your control, you then go talk to the counselors at the school. You go talk to the teachers and activate another layer of protection for your child with the other adults that are there, making those folks aware of what you are seeing and the impact of those messages. I think because it is junior high, adults tend to default to "You'll make it through. Just go to school." But I think they need to understand their need to lean in. Try to use your adolescent experiences to assess your child's experience to activate protection and interception of harmful messages, because they'll hear them again tomorrow. But it's easier to hear them tomorrow if the residue from yesterday isn't still there. When you don't do that, it compounds, and that's how it takes root. So you have to get them engaged in something they enjoy. Help cultivate a place where they're getting love from those peer groups so that their every interaction isn't bringing pain. No matter how shallow the adoration. It also gives them a clique, the jock clique or the band clique, which kind of becomes their family within a family. The bottom line is, every kid is unique, and every parent is unique. There is no cookie-cutter way to raise a child.

I'm not a perfect parent, but I continue to do my best. I was the best parent I could be, and a lot of my parenting was informed by operating in defiance of the perceptions that we would fail. After graduating from high school, Cadence got accepted into NYU's School of Engineering. Upon graduating, she started her career in corporate America and, after COVID, joined me in New York as she continues to build her career.

# Burn Your Cardigan

I've always had a sense of my style, and it is very much a part of my identity. I embrace it fully, and I love it. However, I did not get to this point easily.

When I took the D&I job at Target, I was the fourth person to lead D&I. Mind you, there had been someone in the leadership role of the Office of D&I for the last ten years, but many people thought I was the first because my style was to engage directly with the team rather than through other departments. By communicating this way, I made people feel that I was the first person who had been in the role.

The approach was to advise the business in the background and allow the business to be the face of how the strategy would show up. My entry wasn't quiet, which by now should be no surprise, but in this context, it matters, because my entrance wasn't just loud; it was active. In my first ninety days, I was holding town hall meetings and visiting stores and distribution centers. I took the role very public internally in a way my predecessors hadn't, so everyone thought the position was new. The perception was that I was put into a new position rather than stepping into a position that I was the fourth person to fill. That perception became the trigger for why I worried about my style.

Target had a reputation for being very young and very chic, especially at corporate headquarters. It was very easy to pick out somebody who worked outside of headquarters based on what they were wearing, because it didn't match what merchants and others at headquarters were known for. There was a discomfort that I could see and feel in meetings, common spaces, and informal gatherings.

The D&I team was already in place when I came into the role. I just stepped in to lead it. One of the first things I did was schedule listening sessions with various departments. I created a safe and open forum for them to share. So when I started doing these rounds, I'd show up dressed in slacks, flats, and cardigans—shit I didn't care about and hated wearing. I would come into a meeting and say, "Hi, I am Caroline, and here is my dope strategy for D&I." I would be telling them to be their authentic selves. My job was now promoting authenticity. I was showing up inauthentically from a style perspective, and I was scared about that. I was sitting there saying, "Here's what you need to do to be successful at Target"; all the while, I couldn't stand what I was wearing. I began to feel like I couldn't do my job properly if I didn't like how I looked or if I didn't start to present some sense of personal authenticity.

Within the world of D&I, we're used to hearing about disparities in race, gender, ability, and even sexual orientation. But those were not the things that made me feel like an "other." My otherness was the pressure related to looking different, which was fueled by coming from a field-facing role to a headquarters-facing role. Now, in my role as the leader of D&I for Target, I had to add to my strategy an approach that would mitigate the impact of aesthetic appearances that were outside of the corporate "norm" or what was expected. No one really talked about it, but if you began to look at who was getting promoted, used for campaigns, and discussed as someone with potential for a future within the organization, there was a clear trend. I now had to think about how, across people and processes, I could make sure that the idea of the way you look, the shape of your body, and what kind of clothes you wear did not hinder your success at Target. It was clear to me that it had to start with me. One of the most important things to me was not to ask anybody to do anything that I was not willing to do first.

I had had every possible hairstyle except for locs. I had always wanted locs, but I can't remember who told me or when I was told that they weren't professional or acceptable in corporate America. So my first step in showing up as me was going straight to the barbershop and asking them to cut out my microbraids at the knot and start my locs. I went to the barbershop that evening right after work, because I had to do it when I thought about it or else I would have been too afraid to follow through with it and do it. The next morning, I looked in the mirror and realized that I was a heavyset Black woman with short starter locs, having gone from shoulder-length microbraids overnight. Visually, it was such a drastic change that, when I arrived at work that next day, I was scared to scan my badge to enter the building. In the ten years I'd worked at Target, I had never been afraid to scan my badge. It was like my subconscious was just doing shit based on what it was worried about, and I was watching it like, *Why am I doing this?* I was afraid of what would happen when I showed up with this hair, so when I went to scan my badge, it was triggering, and I hesitated. There was no hair policy at Target, but the unspoken pressure in place to look a certain way most certainly included hair.

That day and for the entire week, I didn't reply to emails. I didn't accept happy hour invitations or answer my phone because I was afraid it was HR calling. I rescheduled most of my meetings and stayed in my office because I didn't want to see people, out of fear of how people would react to my hair. I would rush into my office in the morning, and when the day was over, I would rush out. I was so consumed with fear that every time I saw people talking, I thought they were talking about me. I stopped going to the cafeteria to get lunch and would instead send my admin. That's how psychologically debilitating this was. My behavior was so out of character that people started to suspect that something was wrong with me. Mind you, I wasn't sorry about changing my hair, but I started to think I shouldn't have. This was week one on the job, and while all of this was going on, I finally realized I'd survived week one—with my locs. So I thought, *Cool. I made it.*

At that time, I wasn't a makeup girl, and I didn't wear anything more than eyeliner or some lip gloss. The glam came later, while I was at Essence, but I had always wanted my signature lipstick to be blue. So I purchased blue lipstick from MAC, wore it to work, and nobody gave two hoots. Now I was like, *I've cut my hair, I've worn blue lipstick, and nobody said shit to me about it, good or bad.* They were probably whispering, but nothing "real" happened. I took their silence to mean I was cool, even though I still thought they were talking about me behind my back.

A couple weeks later, I was getting ready one morning for work, and I decided to pull something from the other side of my closet, the non-Target side, and wear something I'd never worn to work before. The thing I chose to wear was a hoodie, which didn't break protocol, but this hoodie had an African mask on the front. I got to work that morning, scanned my badge, got triggered, hesitated, and headed to my office. The crazy thing was that no one ever said anything to me about my hair, my blue lipstick, or the African mask hoodie. I never asked because I was afraid to get an answer. Over the next several weeks, I would wear little things here and there in an attempt to peel back the layers of my "corporate costume."

One morning, I woke up, and I was like, *Fuck it. I'm going H.A.M.!* I went and pulled out the extreme Caroline style. I was done tiptoeing around. Instead of just rolling out my style reveal slowly, I just went all in. This meant day sequins and tulle on a Tuesday and the craziest spectrum of women's size-eleven shoes you can imagine. In addition, after thirty years of being told I needed to wear glasses, I started wearing them, and you know, they were funky. Oh, and I went from blue lipstick to black lipstick, and I still rock black lipstick to this day.

I was a senior officer at a Fortune 100 company, and I was no longer just trying to make a statement; I was owning my style and saying, "This is who the fuck Caroline is!" I even showed up at a board meeting in a dress that had a bit of a Chewbacca vibe. It had a regular shift dress silhouette, but it was fur on fur on fur. When I walked into the meeting with the CEO, his direct reports, and the Target board of directors, they didn't say anything about what I was wearing, but they gave pretty clear top-to-bottom looks. So to break the ice, I said, "Yes, this is Chewbacca chic." They all just laughed, and that was that.

The next day, when I was presenting the company's D&I strategy to the board, I wore a dress-and-sneaker ensemble, and I sat right next to the Target CEO to present. After my presentation, I stood to leave, and Brian Cornell (Target's CEO) said, "I like your shoes, Caroline." With that one statement, he demonstrated what it looks like to drive inclusion through influence. That was the last day I ever worried about what I looked like when I came to work.

A lot of the journey thus far had been about worrying about being authentic in my job and how that would impact doing my job. As I continued to own my style, I encountered additional impact that I did not anticipate when another Black leader in the organization came to tell me that because I decided to wear locs, she now felt safe to wear braids at work. It caught me off guard because I had been so focused on my job that I hadn't realized how much of the way that I looked impacted how other people in the company felt they could look at work. This was the point in which I fully understood how my aesthetic was connected to my purpose and a critical component of inspiring others. This moment was transformative and prompted a decision that would liberate me in ways I never thought possible.

Throughout my journey, there have been times when I lost touch with my true self and my authenticity. This was glaringly apparent during my early days at Target. When I was in the distribution center, I tried to copy the actions of the successful people around me, believing it would lead to my success. I shopped at stores like New York & Company, which used to be the Lerner Shops and then Lerners. They cater to women in corporate America and sell cardigans, twinsets, slacks, you name it. Choosing that wardrobe is safe in a corporate setting. If you're not into suits, a cardigan or twinset with slacks is the go-to corporate look. I purchased a ton of cardigans, even though I despised them. They weren't my taste or my style at all. But for me, there was safety in figuring out: "Okay, Jenny wears cardigans and keeps getting promoted. I should wear cardigans too." My closet was full of cardigans. I'm a big-chested girl. The buttons wouldn't stay closed, they were weird on my shoulders, and they had never been right for me.

Now that I was in my more authentic aesthetic, I made up my mind to give away everything in my wardrobe that did not represent "me," except for the cardigans. Those cardigans had been a part of my unhealthy life for so long that just giving them away or tossing them out didn't feel monumental enough considering the turning point I was reaching. I needed a more tangible and significant way to announce this change and mourn the fact that I'd been wearing things I despised just to get by. At this point, I'd already donated much of my wardrobe to Goodwill, but I kept those damn cardigans around—I owned more cardigans in my wardrobe than any other kind of clothing, and I loathed them. I could've given them away, but the emotional trauma made me feel like destroying them. Do you remember the scene in the movie *Waiting to Exhale* where Angela Bassett sets the car on fire? Stay in that moment, except this was Maple Grove, Minnesota, and there were no mountains. There was none of that. There was no car. There was none of that backdrop; there was only grass or concrete. Concrete doesn't burn, right?

I lived in a townhome on a cul-de-sac with no cars, just cement. So I went outside and built a pile of cardigans. I doused them with lighter fluid, thinking it would speed up the burn. And that was it; I set them ablaze. I thought, *I'll just watch until the fire goes out.* I knew there might be some remnants. I planned to sweep those bits into a bag and toss them. So I was standing there watching them burn, right, and I heard this fire truck roll up. I was like, *Someone done called the fire department?* I was deep in my own world, so even though I knew they were probably coming for me, it was all about the experience. I stayed focused on my thing. I wasn't going to put out the fire or run away all scared. Nah, I wasn't afraid at all.

I felt a bit of this strange kind of satisfaction, like "They're here," to use a familiar phrase from little Carol Anne Freeling in the film *Poltergeist*. The moment had that sort of vibe going on.

So these four firemen hopped out of the fire truck, and I was just waving at them. They could tell it wasn't anything serious, so they came over, asking if I'd dumped my man or something. Honestly, I didn't know which "him" they were referring to at first. I put two and two together and figured they thought I was burning my boyfriend's or husband's stuff like some angry woman. I was like, "Nah, it isn't about a breakup or anything like that; I just wanted to torch my cardigans."

"Why are you burning your sweaters?" they asked me.

"'Cause I can't stand them" was my response.

And again, they were like, "Uh . . . why?"

So I said to them straight up, "Isn't it obvious? Can't stand them 'cause they're cardigans."

I didn't give them any more explanation than that—I just kept answering their questions, really chill. Two firefighters stuck around and chitchatted with me while the other two returned to their truck and got their fire hose out. They must've thought I was straight-up loco! But they never said it. The pair just tried to keep me talking while their buddies put the fire out and tidied up the mess. They hadn't mentioned that they would clean up, but they did it anyway. Once they finished, they hit me with a "Have a good day, ma'am."

I said, "Deuces, fellas!" and made my way back inside.

I like rituals, meaning I like to commemorate things. The way I operate in the world requires that I put a pin in pivotal moments. Burning my cardigans is an example. When I set those sweaters ablaze, it was a statement about who I'd decided I was going to be in the world. Target wasn't even the focus anymore. This was about me and what I wanted the future me to be. I had no idea where the future was going to take me, but what I knew for sure was that whatever the future held, I was going to show up as my 100 percent authentic self.

After all of this, my style became much more than just a way of being or personal expression for me. My look was now the reason people believed Target was serious about D&I. While this was an outstanding turn of events, there was still another hurdle to crush. I was the vice president of diversity and inclusion, and I now had to take a company-sanctioned headshot, which I had never done. The normal process is, once you achieve the position of vice president and/or have a heavily external-facing job, Target organizes and manages your headshot.

Specific guidelines are issued, like no patterns, focusing on red, incorporating a little khaki, styling your hair in a way that won't change much, and keeping it business casual. I looked at the guideline sheet and laughed. There were, like, two things on the list of guidelines that even sort of made sense for the way I dressed, and not a single thing made sense for my hair. I showed up on the day of the shoot wearing a gray shirt, with my hair and makeup the way I love it, locs, blue lipstick, and all. I knew what was going to happen, and I could feel all that passive-aggressive energy the moment I crossed paths with the communications team (COMS). One of them approached me with the not-so-subtle-yet-sickly-sweet "Oh, is that what you're wearing?"

"Yes," I said.

To which she replied, "You're not changing?"

"No," I answered.

"Did you receive and read the criteria?" she asked, now somewhat befuddled.

I told her I had received it and read it, but I hadn't taken it as a mandate. At this point, she didn't know what to do, because she had no authority over me; she simply covered my department. She then turned to the photographer and said to him, right in front of me and in full earshot, "Do the best you can. If we have to schedule another one, we will."

The photographer looked at me nervously, and I said to him, in front of everyone, "Do the best you can. There won't be another one." So we did the shoot, and I did what I do. The photographer did his thing, and that was that. Three days later, my boss called and asked how the shoot went. I said that it went great. My boss explained that there had been some "feedback" that I hadn't seemed to be within the guidelines of the issued criteria. Clearly, this had been escalated from COMS, and my boss was now coming to my office. When she arrived, I asked if she'd seen the photos, and she said she hadn't. I would have offered to send them to her, but I hadn't seen them either. So now COMS was giving feedback on photos that neither I nor my boss had seen.

I suggested to my boss that she request the photos from COMS so we could both see them. In the back of my mind, I thought COMS had deleted the file to force a reschedule. Instead, two days later, after receiving the photos, my boss called and said, "I like them. We're not doing a reshoot." I was no longer afraid. This was the moment I really started to own it even more. I got obnoxious about it. This was when my headshots became activism.

I have been photographed for headshots many times since then, and every one of them has been a form of activism. I decided I was only going to take headshots that reflected the space I was in at that time, and that remains my aesthetic. But the struggle is real, and to this day, whenever my official headshot is sent out, nine times out of ten, the prospective client or organization will write back and ask if I have a *professional one* because my high-resolution, HD, professionally photographed headshot doesn't meet their criteria. When this request comes in, I will ask my team to request a copy of the criteria. Rarely have any criteria been sent, and no one has ever canceled a speaking engagement, interview, or appearance because I refused to change my headshot. The fact is, if you can't handle my official headshot, you sure as hell won't like the live experience.

Once that Target moment happened, I became indignant about it. To be clear, I don't do crazy headshots just to do crazy headshots. Every one of them is an intentional and effective form of covert activism. I refuse to compromise simply because the way I present makes other people uncomfortable. It is important to me to fight for the ones who don't feel like they can. Once you allow the first change to your headshot for reasons other than the technical quality of the shot, you open the floodgates to manipulate or manage your image to fit someone else's standard. That's why, as it pertains to this subject, nah, I won't change.

I was recently asked what I would say to someone up-and-coming who may feel like they don't possess the agency to buck convention. I would tell anyone, particularly young Black women, to do you from the beginning. Don't wait until you have to fight for your authenticity. Once you've attained a position, job, or promotion, that activates scrutiny and management of your image. The pressure to conform isn't less; it's more. Be your authentic self from the jump.

When I was below the vice president level, no one was managing my headshot. No one cared. I was the one who looked around me and decided what I had to do to be accepted. The crazy thing about it is, I probably had more agency back then to do whatever the hell I wanted and to wear whatever the hell I wanted to wear. If I had presented my authentic self from the jump, I would have saved myself a lot of heartache, anxiety, and stress, but I couldn't see that because I was too busy wearing cardigans.

When I figured it out, my performance and productivity went from 50 percent to 150 percent. The percentage of energy I poured into worrying about what I was wearing, what my hair looked like, and my body image, along with what I thought everyone was thinking about them, was now freed up to propel me to the top of my game.

Once you let go of trying to be who you think others want you to be and step into your authenticity, you will experience a freedom that will show up in every area of your life. Some people will be uncomfortable, and it will express itself in a myriad of ways. When you make a decision not to conform, they will either fall off, or the universe will propel you to something better. The universe always confirms that which is right. Either way, you will have stepped into a new dimension of possibility, creativity, opportunity, and flow that will be 100 percent authentically yours.

**"If you can't be who you are where you are,
don't change who you are; change where you are."**

# This Ain't Scrabble

I stepped into the diversity and inclusion role with a mix of anger and frustration because it seemed like folks in the industry believed they could change the game by simply shuffling letters around. This isn't a game of Scrabble. You don't win at creating lasting change by how you arrange letters; you make a difference by how you empower people and transform environments to genuinely meet one another halfway. Here's what I mean. After affirmative action, the "new" work was defined as diversity and inclusion. In the decade since, minimum progress has been made, yet it continues to be renamed, as though renaming it will accelerate results. Over the years, here are some of the other organizational and industry names that have been created that may sound familiar: Adding the word "equity" to make it "DEI." Putting the *I* before the *D* to communicate "inclusion" before "diversity." Then there is the addition of the word "belonging" under the pretense that "inclusion" was an incomplete thought and "belonging" was the destination. Adding "justice" to "equity, diversity, and inclusion." Taking the words "diversity" and "inclusion" out altogether and calling it "equity and belonging." Combining any mix of these letters with other functional names, like "culture" and "philanthropy." Also, the push to add "race" and "accessibility" to it turned the acronym into READI.

Here we are over a decade later, and what's really changed? Not much. Renaming doesn't get the work done. Action does. Real change doesn't come from catchy acronyms or buzzwords; it comes from hard, consistent work. It's about holding systems accountable and equipping people with what they need to succeed. It's about changing the everyday reality for folks on the ground, not just the words we use in boardrooms. I came into this field to do more than just move letters around. That meant pushing for policies that mattered, practices that made a difference, and a culture that truly included everyone. We didn't need another term to trumpet out on social media; we needed results that you could feel, that you could see, that made life better for everyone—not just Black people but all people. But for me, my focus is especially on Black people. That's the work that still needs to be done. Despite this constant reconfiguration of terms—D&I, DEI, READI, as though they're pieces in an eternally shifting puzzle—the reality for Black folks is still what it is. These acronyms are little more than ornamental facades. True transformation doesn't manifest within the confines of a catchy acronym; it's not conjured by the rebranding of corporate-speak. I understand corporate verbiage; I've spent my life in that world. I can talk the talk. I know how to operate in that construct, but they are just words if there is no commitment to change. Real, tangible progress doesn't happen by just giving the problem a new anthem, acronym, or soapbox to stand on.

It's about action, and until the actions align with the words, until they resonate with the force and conviction that outstrip any linguistic flourish, the acronym remains insufficient for the underserved, ignored, and disenfranchised. It's not about the letters we see; it's about the changes we feel. If change and progress aren't measurable, are they even real? That's what matters to me now and what mattered to me when I stepped into the D&I role at Target.

When I took on the D&I role, I was immediately bombarded with suggestions and ideas about changing the department's name, as if a new label would somehow give it gravitas or deliver better results. I resisted every push to go down that path. To me, it was crystal clear: rearranging the letters wasn't going to change the nature of the task at hand. I had no interest in wasting my time evangelizing a new set of initials. My focus was on the real, tangible work that needed to start—breaking down barriers, building equity, and creating an environment where everyone had the opportunity to succeed. That's where I wanted to channel my energy. From my perspective, everything else was just "doing something" for the sake of saying that you were "doing something." I had a strategy to ground my efforts in reality. First, I needed to listen—really listen—to the team's voices to understand their feelings about diversity and inclusion at Target. Because I had spent time with Kim Strong, my predecessor in this role, I had pivotal information that I leveraged.

Kim Strong—a Black woman who had been with Target for nearly three decades—became my champion. She was brilliant at building relationships and had a deep passion for developing people. If you were at Target, you'd have likely seen Kim offering a word of wisdom, encouragement, guidance, or support to anyone she came across. She was well respected and influential, especially in the stores. I had met her before at different events, but when she took the position of vice president of D&I at headquarters, and I decided that I wanted that role, our relationship evolved, and we connected on a new level. "Sponsorship" is a word often batted around in the business world, but it's essentially about having a heavyweight in your corner—someone to help guide and elevate you. I hadn't thought much about it until Kim declared that she was my sponsor at a Target D&I event. That's when it really clicked; I needed to understand what sponsorship really meant, because she was ready to be that person for me.

When I look back, I can see that trying to study the concept of sponsorship was unnecessary, because Kim's actions spoke volumes. I remember a conversation early on, when Kim discussed with me how I was viewed by our HR department. She wasn't obligated to do that; our professional lines did not intersect in that way. I wasn't on her team, and I didn't report to her. Yet she took it upon herself, because as my sponsor, her goal was to ensure I was well informed, vigilant, and fully equipped for promotion.

Kim's approach to sponsorship at Target was both strategic and intentional, and it had a profound impact on my career journey. She didn't just give generic advice; she took a vested interest in my personal growth within the company. With a keen understanding that career advancement goes hand in hand with strategic knowledge, Kim intentionally shared the kind of insights and intel usually reserved for those in the higher echelons of leadership. Regularly, she shared with me important company updates that were normally reserved for senior leadership so that I could demonstrate that I understood the enterprise company strategy and priorities, which is an important part of exceeding at the next level. This allowed me to tailor my actions and decisions to align with Target's overarching strategies—something that is vital not just in advancing within a specific role but in any career and, indeed, in life itself. This kind of genuine sponsorship is rare but so important in navigating the complexities of a corporation like Target.

When someone like Kim steps up, be ready. I knew what I wanted. I knew where I wanted to go. I'd followed the trajectory of my map and even jumped over steps to get to where I was. When the opportunity presented itself, I was ready, and the sponsor appeared. She equipped me with the right information at the right time. She helped me understand the dynamics of the business, which allowed me to leverage that understanding and make impactful contributions. Kim's intentional guidance gave me a path to opportunities and advancement that might otherwise have remained out of my reach. Part of the intent of this book is to be that for you so you can be that for someone else. It is important to note that Kim knew my goal was to one day step into her role. She gave me opportunities that challenged and extended my skill set and capabilities. She included me in critical meetings and introduced me to the "right" people in the world of D&I, which not only prepared me for future responsibilities but also positioned me as a credible successor. Had Kim not decided to be my sponsor and backed it up with actions that matched her words, my journey would have been much different. When my promotion was announced, Kim marked the moment with a gesture I'll never forget. She framed the announcement email and gave it to me as a reminder of the achievement—an achievement not everyone gets to celebrate. Kim's impact on my journey is something I carry with me with deep appreciation.

I wasn't a career D&I person. I didn't come from a traditional diversity, equity, and inclusion (DEI) path. While my background wasn't rooted in traditional DEI, I brought fresh eyes and a unique perspective to the table, shaped by my time in the nonprofit sector. Back in the day, before I stepped into the corporate world, I was all about community organizing. I'd literally hit the pavement, knocking on doors, chatting with folks to get the "real" on what they needed. It was about getting folks to speak up at town hall meetings and making sure we got help to where it was needed most. My approach was down-to-earth, relatable, and accessible. I also wanted to build confidence in the community so they would know they mattered to me and that I was going to always do my best for them. I wanted them to know I would keep my word, even if I couldn't always do everything.

When I joined the D&I team at Target, I brought that same vibe with me. I made sure we kept our ears to the ground and our hearts open so we could get what our customers and employees were about. This wasn't your typical corporate playbook—it was about keeping it real and making sure everyone felt heard and valued, which is pretty much the secret sauce to a great workplace and happy customers. My time in nonprofit youth development was all about equipping young folks with the skills and behaviors they'd need to thrive later in life. That's really what inclusion and empathy are about in a company setting—helping employees develop in ways that benefit both them and the organization in the long term. Collaboration was key in the nonprofit sector, and it was no different in D&I work. Bringing different groups together to amplify their impacts was something I was doing long before I stepped into the corporate world.

In my first ninety days in my role as chief diversity officer, I went directly to the team to hear how they felt about diversity and inclusion at Target. I set up town halls focused on discussions with employees on Target's policies, vision, goals, thoughts, and perspective in the D&I space. Then I immersed myself in benchmarking how diversity and inclusion were realized in other industries and companies. Next was identifying what overall best practices were not present in Target's strategy. The last piece was researching how to specifically define what success looked like. It was essential not only to have a vision but also to establish measurable indicators of our progress. It hit me right away that many employees didn't even know we had a D&I department or what it was about. So my job was to make D&I understandable and relevant—to define who we were, what we did, why it mattered, and a way to measure if we were actually making a difference.

When it came time to benchmark D&I practices, I reached out to people who had my role at other retail companies and organizations who managed and assessed the success of diversity and inclusion at companies. I engaged with consultants to understand the options I had for operational frameworks to move the work forward. I was building a playbook based on real relationships and proven strategies.

My conclusion after the benchmarking was that Target had the right intent and environment to move the needle, not just for itself but for the retail and the broader D&I industries. But to get there, we needed to sharpen our focus. What were missing were a simplified business case, a definition of prioritized goals across business and team, a mechanism for measuring and defining the KPI that would outline success, and the need to adjust the D&I team from advisors to accountability partners and move our team from invisible to visible. I vehemently believed that we had the talent in-house to make this happen without outside consultants.

A significant hurdle that D&I practitioners' efforts face is the lack of support and/or direct access to their CEOs. That's where the real power to drive change lies. The reason it matters is because of the authority and influence that the CEO has to make the company behave a certain way. One of the things that I am most grateful for is that I never experienced any kind of misalignment or lack of support from Brian Cornell. Brian, who was, at that time, the new CEO. He was Target's first-ever external CEO in the history of the company. Brian never wavered in his support of D&I and frankly in his support of me. Brian's support was paramount to the success of my time as chief diversity officer, and his support was genuine. He was more interested in exacting a policy and a set of procedures that would move the needle in D&I inside of Target than showing up in the top ten of someone's survey. I respected that, and he respected me and gave me the space, time, and exposure to do what I needed to do.

Retail is a place where people can get jobs without a college degree, where people can work multiple hours and get hired at age sixteen. His goal was to watch the payroll funds flow through the communities it served, and the folks who worked in the stores came from the surrounding communities. He wanted our presence to have reciprocal benefits. However, Brian's approach, though genuine, was not altogether altruistic. That is to say that Target winning retail was the salient point.

Brian came to Target at a very similar time in the business as I would later enter Essence. After a major scandal. The optics were bad; the reality was worse. As the company's first external CEO,

Brian's expectations were high. He stepped into the role after a major data breach, an uncertain expansion into Canada, and underperforming domestic operations. Despite all of this, he quickly and enthusiastically engaged with me to discuss the vision for Target to become a leader in corporate diversity and inclusion. Our initial discussions centered on the D&I strategy, and I was impressed by the ease with which I could secure time with him. There was never a time when Brian was inaccessible to me. As the D&I initiative grew, our interactions became more frequent, and our dynamic evolved into an enriching mentorship. Brian was genuinely interested in me as an individual—my family, aspirations, strengths, and areas for improvement. His guidance became a cornerstone of my personal and professional growth. His advocacy for our D&I initiatives was unwavering, and his willingness to engage with me on a personal level was a mark of his character. He had an extraordinary ability to identify potential in me that I hadn't recognized in myself, and this belief in my capabilities anchored our relationship. After a crucial period when my mental health necessitated a leave of absence, Brian was the first to suggest that my return to work had been premature. He provided the support and the safety I needed to take additional time off. He insisted that I take more time, and not for one second was I in fear for my job or my status in the company. That spoke volumes to me about who this man was.

At other times, it was him offering psychological safety by determining how to interact with employees who disagreed with how I was driving D&I and wanted reprieve by talking to him about it. He stood firm, not deviating from the path we had set, a decision that further solidified our trust in each other. When I was looking to expand my role with a new challenge, his support with an internal search as well as external engagement defined a level of trust with a mentor, friend, CEO, and colleague that I had never experienced in my professional career, and that was demonstrated by the fact that what Caroline needed versus what Target needed was often the place where Brian would be team Caroline.

Target was a fifty-year-old retail giant built on precision—clear goals, defined behaviors, timely metrics, and disciplined governance and enforcement of the achievement of those goals. Success in D&I required that I use the same approach to articulate where we would be focused across the company from a D&I perspective. So over the next few years, we redefined the D&I business intelligence, analytics, resources, and reporting. We developed, defined, and implemented the first set of company-wide goals tied to the business, teams, and reputation. We attached compensation consequences to the most senior-level roles in the company to reinforce that participation in achieving our goals was not optional and that not meeting those goals would impact pay. Part of the way that the compensation was set up was that the senior leaders were held accountable for how the entire function, not just their particular departments, performed on the goals. This was important, because it required that each of the leaders cared about and supported the D&I performances of the other departments in the function, not just their own, which ensured that they were collaborating on behalf of all of the employees within their business. The goals were three-year objectives emphasizing being realistic about how long change takes. We developed a matrix for how the broader company ecosystem would align to support achieving those goals. For example, I spent a lot of time with the learning and development part of the company defining a company-wide inclusion acumen curriculum for each business function based on what their goals were. Another example was working with marketing, merchandising, philanthropy, and supplier diversity to articulate how we would ensure that our products, messages, and guest-facing experiences reflected the demographics of where our stores were located. We simplified the business case and stated that 75 percent of the US was within ten miles of a Target store and one click away from Target.com. Our ability to deliver what they wanted would increase brand affinity and competitive advantage. After the first set of three-year goals were achieved—i.e., all of the milestones, etc.—we then proceeded to define the next set of goals more aggressively. Additionally, we chose to partner with other retailers through the Retail Industry Leaders Association (RILA), a trade organization in the retail industry that Brian was the chair of at that time. He established the first-ever RILA Diversity and Inclusion Committee, focused on changing the diversity and inclusion results across the entire retail industry. He appointed me to lead that committee and effort. One of the most interesting things that came with being appointed to lead the RILA Diversity and Inclusion Committee was that the people we were working with represented all of Target's competitors. I remember asking Brian how to handle teaching what we had done with D&I at Target to be successful with sharing information that could compromise our competitive advantage in the retail industry. One of the things that Brian shared in response was that in his role as RILA chair, the power of the entire retail industry was what he wanted to harness and amplify. The number of employees in the retail industry at the time was over 17 million, which meant the impact economically, communally, and environmentally that we could make if we positioned both the companies and their employees in retail to be the best in class in diversity and inclusion would impact neighborhoods, families, and legacies for generations to come. Therefore, Brian's guidance to me was to give them everything we legally could that would accelerate their business results through diversity and inclusion. Then we would be at the same starting line to compete, and may the best company win. Brian's point was based on his confidence that Target would continue to perform in excellence in retail, and he didn't want to win against companies that had a diversity and inclusion deficiency. He wanted to win against companies that were performing at their best as well. Hence why the work of the RILA Diversity and Inclusion Committee was some of the most rewarding work I got to do in my role.

One of the benefits of the RILA role I had was that I was able to get a bird's-eye view of the diversity and inclusion strategy at multiple retailers. I was proud of the progress we made at Target and wanted to continue to drive it, but I needed a new challenge in the role. In the first four years, we'd built a new strategy, built a new business case, launched the retail diversity strategy under RILA, developed our D&I company goals, tied them to compensation, implemented the first set, met the goals within the first three years, then developed and launched the second set for the next three years. All of that happened between 2014 and 2018. I was very satisfied with the work we did, and I still see the fruit of our efforts within the organization today.

*Now what?* I knew I was headed into a rinse-and-repeat moment. The challenge and the "newness" had gone out of it, and I would soon enter a "maintenance," or managing and governing, phase of my time at Target, and I tend to get distracted when things become status quo. It came as a surprise to no one when I began to express my desire to be differently challenged. I'd been at the company for ten years, and I wasn't ready to leave the diversity and inclusion area. My external reputation and visibility were on the rise because of numerous internal and external requests to tell the story of Target's diversity and inclusion culture. The request came from conferences, other companies, D&I organizations, external Target events, etc. I think if I had been willing to leave D&I, I might have found a different job internally faster. Frankly, I wanted to build a successor. I knew that D&I was at the place where I no longer needed to be in every piece of the minutiae, which was great because I needed a new problem to solve. The internal search was on for me to add things to my plate; headhunters were continually inquiring about my interest in D&I positions at other companies. Previously, I would ignore them, but one day, I decided to call one of them back. Because of the relationship I had built with Brian and others, I didn't feel comfortable continuing external conversations without informing my internal supporters.

Now let me say this: I would not advise anyone to do that in a regular corporate environment. Telling your boss and your boss's boss you are interviewing for external positions will most likely be seen as a threat. I was very fortunate to have a relationship born of trust and open communication with my internal supporters that welcomed this type of interaction. Unless you can confirm that you have the same, be cautious about sharing external pursuits internally.

The guidance that I got from my internal supporters as I went on this journey was focused on a few areas. The first one was understanding the board of directors in any public company and researching any activist shareholders. Another one was understanding the state of performance of all parts of the business, not just the ones that were underperforming. The last one was understanding the stage of maturity that each company was in in your area of expertise. So those things, in addition to the guidance I was getting from headhunters of where my Target experience would be beneficial, gave me a pretty good view of what types of roles in D&I were good options for me. Those external engagements gave me a good construct for the different D&I roles in retail. Here is what I discovered.

First, there were different types of retailers when it came to D&I, and there were different things that differentiated them, such as whether they were US-based or global (because D&I means something different outside the US). The next thing was where the Office of D&I reported departmentally (because the effectiveness of D&I work is impacted by the internal clout of the department it reports to). The third one was understanding what level of D&I maturity I wanted to spend my time operating in, because it is important for me to understand the components—whether we wanted to start a D&I program at a company, continue one, or evolve one. Clearly understanding the primary products of the retailer to determine whether a business case for D&I could be created. Finally, understanding the difference between a franchised or corporate-owned retailer, because the level of ownership a corporation has over all its locations significantly influences alignment regarding strategy, enforcement of KPIs, and a consistent inclusive culture.

I wasn't engaging only externally in conversations about my next challenge; there were internal conversations as well. The internal path was about finding functions that I could add to my responsibilities and still keep D&I. For example, philanthropy, culture, sustainability, talent, and public affairs. And on similar timing to the external search, none of the internal options panned out. Therefore, in partnership with my internal supporters, we decided to pause searching for a little while.

At this point, Brian told me he wanted me to do more externally. He said he wasn't comfortable putting me out front while I was looking externally, but now that the search had ended, he wanted me to be more forward-facing. The Talent Acquisitions Department at Target does a series of conferences across America called Target Lab. The conferences include workshops, a meal, a keynote speaker, and interviews. Brian asked me to travel with Target Lab and serve as the keynote speaker. The rest of the world discovered me when I began to travel as the keynote speaker for Target Lab.

# Lookin' [GI]Ass

By now you can see how much of my career was driven by my maps. Considering that my second map was accomplished years before I thought it would be, I felt the urge to create another one, even though I had only been in my current role for a few years. What eventually became my Architecture of Authenticity workshops and courses began as a doodle that I created one day when I was bored at a conference but was thinking through what corporate D&I executives do once they get to the top levels of the function. What I learned after taking the role in D&I was that most corporate D&I executives that transition out of their companies either start or join a D&I consulting firm, write a book and/or a bunch of white papers, promote the concepts of their books or firms, attend conferences or give speeches and workshops, and sell their frameworks back to the corporate industries they used to work in.

So, armed with the knowledge of the typical career path, I started to think about what my unique offering would be if I followed the natural trajectory of corporate D&I executives. I wasn't in a rush because I was only a couple of years into my role, but I wanted to be prepared, because this was going to be the first career map that would take me out of Target.

The journey that I had been on to have a more authentic aesthetic impacted more people than I realized, while at that same time, it increased my productivity. With that realization in mind, those outcomes became a good starting point for what I could see as two key factors (authenticity and productivity) for the base of what I would share if I became a consultant. The reason why this made sense was because as I continued to be known in the industry, I was constantly observing and experiencing D&I professionals who were the least authentic people I had ever met. When I would see my colleagues at industry events, I was always tickled at how much people who worked in D&I complimented me for being real and different. It took me back to the reason why I started working on my aesthetic: because I now had a job where I was supposed to tell people that they could be authentic at work. I was worried that if I didn't show up authentically, it would be in conflict with what my job was. Because of my experience sitting in a room with a whole bunch of corporate D&I executives, I thought that should be the place where I would run into a significant number of people who were comfortable living in their authenticity. As I noticed that authenticity was unique in the place where I expected it to be abundant, I determined that the way that I would teach D&I would be anchored in first teaching people how to be authentic. That is where my third career map started.

I started by reflecting on my personal and professional journeys before Target and while at Target. A few things became clear, which led to my authenticity framework. The first part centered on helping people understand what they were born to do in the world, because when I looked at my journey, my authenticity was anchored in the point in which I understood my purpose. It contained three parts. It started with understanding what you did well and what you didn't do well by talking individually to people who knew you differently, so you could see the theme of your strengths and weaknesses come to life. The next part was leaning into what you learned regarding what you were best at and creating an audacious agenda for how you were going to offer it to the world. Third was training yourself to listen to the voice of dissent with the same energy with which you listened to the voice of affirmation. Those three parts made up the center of the framework and were the activities that helped someone understand their purpose. The second section focused on the sequence for entering the workplace as you manifested your purpose. This part did not contain any radical ideas; it was more about the order in which you did them. It started with being exceptionally good at your job, as authenticity should not be a substitute for performance. Next was relationship capital, which focused on the key groups of people that impacted how your performance was assessed. The third one was focused on offering intrusive insight into the business based on who you were in your past experiences, and the last step was about self-advocacy for the types of roles you wanted to have in the company. The last part of the framework was guardrails that served as the rules for coexisting in an environment where everybody's authenticity was maximized.

I shared my framework with a consultant, Glenn Llopis, who had worked with the previous Target D&I team. He had served in a mentor capacity as I was learning the D&I work. I originally showed him the framework so he could help me identify whether this would be a unique offering in the D&I space. As he looked at it, he stated very clearly to me, "This is not a career map; this is a product," and vowed to prove it to me.

"You need to tell people about this." I told him he was BS-ing me. So he invited me to present it at his conference, on a panel that included Magic Johnson. He said, "After you present it, then you can tell me I'm BS-ing you." That was the first time I presented the Architecture of Authenticity publicly, and as Glenn had promised, the reaction from the audience affirmed that the framework was unique, simple, clear, practical, and game-changing.

Target was continually recruiting talent nationally; although there was value in recruiting talent at diversity conferences, Target wanted to own a more direct link with its diverse candidates. So the Talent Acquisitions team launched a proprietary set of regional recruiting experiences called Target Lab. The locations were selected based on the diversity of the demographics of the residents. The experiences often included workshops, keynote speakers, and on-site interviews for roles across the company. Because I was in a D&I role and this was a diversity-recruiting initiative, my team was often involved in the details of the planning of these events, and I also became the consistent keynote speaker for each one. It was necessary to brand each component of the event to keep the process repeatable. Therefore, my keynote needed to be labeled, and because it was simply me capturing my personal and professional experiences, titling it the "Architecture of Authenticity" made sense and integrated well into the event.

The focus of Target Lab was not trying to get people to come work at Target; the intent was to help them develop a deeper understanding of who they were and to help them determine whether Target was the right place for them. Naturally, my keynote address at each Target Lab offered numerous opportunities to test and learn how the framework was received by the audience. What became clear was that the framework's principles could be used at any job and in every walk of life. This wasn't about giving information so specific to Target that it was of little to no value anywhere else. We wanted people to leave Target Lab with information that they could use whether they ever came to work at Target, and I believe that this was one of the loudest moments tied to my desire to get everybody to live authentically through activating their purpose.

Glenn was right; this was bigger than a career map. The location, size, and composition of the crowd didn't matter; it was having the intended effect. Even the Target employees who heard it repeatedly were taking it in. Because this was being presented regionally with a focus on diverse candidates, word of how impactful the framework was began spreading across corporate America. So what started to happen was people would say, "You have to get to Target Lab and hear this." This created a followership at Target Lab of people who weren't even looking for a job; they just came to Target Lab to hear the framework. What I appreciated about it was that I was able to ask the people who would talk to me after each presentation what resonated with them. That was the most valuable set of feedback in refining the Architecture of Authenticity. If only one person got something out of what I was teaching, and that changed their life, I had done my job. I focused on delivering the message and let the universe do the work of getting it to the person who needed to hear it.

I live in reverent fear of my purpose. People often talk about God in this way. I revere God, and the word "revere" is crucial. I am afraid to not do what I am supposed to or say what I feel when I am out front, because my disobedience could mean that someone missed the one thing I might have said that would have made all the difference to them. When I talk about living in reverent fear of my purpose, it means accepting it fully, understanding there is something bigger than me to deliver, and staying committed to delivering it, regardless of how I feel or whether I want to. I don't get to not do it, because I know how impactful it is. Even when I'm scared, it pushes me to do things I may not otherwise choose to do. That's why I tell people I'm not confident. I'm courageous. Those are two different things. I'm not afraid of my destiny. No. I'm leaning into my fear heavily, blindly. My role is to help people understand that fearlessness is not the answer. Do it scared. Don't NOT do it. Do it scared. Somebody needs it. That's why I tell people, "It ain't about you." This has nothing to do with you. This is for the one person who needs it. They'll say a speech changed their life, saved their life. And when that's the kind of response you get to things you said out of reverence, purpose has a way of finding you. By now the reactions to my Architecture of Authenticity talks were so intense that they satisfied the antsy part of me and, more importantly, gave me reinforcement that I was on the right path.

One of the things that I continue to learn is that more people are watching than I can see. I had never attended the Essence Festival, so when Jameel Spencer asked me to host a panel there in 2019, I accepted that there was something about the way I had been showing up that led to this opportunity, and I wanted to do it. The Essence brand had been recently acquired by Richelieu Dennis and his family from Time Warner. This transaction put the Essence brand back under Black ownership after two decades with the Time Warner company. Rich was the founder of SheaMoisture, a multicultural beauty brand he and his family started twenty-five years before they bought Essence. The success of the SheaMoisture brand was anchored in the retail partnership they had with the Target Corporation for fifteen years. The sale of the SheaMoisture brand to Unilever is what created the capital that the Dennis family used to buy Essence in 2018. Ironically, I had worked at Target for fifteen years, and the Dennis family had worked with Target for fifteen years, and we had never met.

Jameel called while I was at Cannes Lions, which is an international festival of creativity, where the chief creative officer of Target, Todd Waterbury, and I were presenting the inclusive children's clothing line Target developed called Cat & Jack. The Cat & Jack line was specifically created with accessibility ports and other modifications that aided children with particular illnesses or disabilities to have clothing that was fun and comfortable and allowed them to still leverage the medical aids on their bodies that they needed to stay healthy. As a proof point that inclusion creates business results, Cat & Jack became one of the highest-performing apparel brands in the company in its first two years.

Because of the timing, I ended up having to travel to New Orleans only a few days after I returned from France. The panel I was hosting focused on inclusivity style and casting in the entertainment world. As I was in the green room preparing, Jameel brought Rich Dennis and Emmet Dennis to say hello. They were confused by the fact that we had never met; their opening statement was "Where was Target hiding you?" We were only able to spend barely twenty minutes together, and when I opened the panel with a quote from a Nat Turner documentary, the only person in the audience who clapped was Rich. At that point, I realized our brains operated the same way. I spent the rest of the weekend enjoying the Essence Festival, and I did not see Rich or Emmet again for the rest of the weekend.

Because of my role in D&I and having met Rich, who had worked with Target previously, he began to invite me to different Essence events to see what partnership opportunities might exist for Target. Rich invited me to attend the Essence Full Circle Festival in Ghana at the end of 2019, and it remains one of the most impactful experiences of my professional life. Ghana was celebrating the year of return. The idea behind this event was to connect a large group of African Americans with their roots in Ghana. Beyond understanding the details of the transatlantic slave trade, the experience was designed to reconnect the legacies of African kingdoms and those who were the descendants of those captured and enslaved and brought to the West. By showcasing life on the continent—the villages, kingdoms, chiefs, and economies—the festival intended to renew and provide an understanding of how powerful the Global Black community is by visiting one of its places of origin. Had COVID not happened, the intent in 2020 had been to bring Africans to the United States to understand the story of what happened with those who were enslaved and brought to the US. It would have been focused on the understanding of what the transatlantic slave trade ignited by highlighting the multiple centuries of oppression that defined the journey from enslavement to full citizenship, including the Emancipation Proclamation, Jim Crow, the Civil Rights Movement, Black Lives Matter, and today. That story was never fully understood by those who were left behind on the African continent. This was the genesis of the new Essence Ventures mission: to connect the disconnected diaspora and create Global Black wealth.

There were at least one hundred individuals who participated in the Full Circle Festival. The group consisted of people of all ages, from children as young as ten to respected elders. Tina Knowles brought students from her Where Art Can Occur (WACO) Theater Center as a part of her program's commitment to connecting young children to the diaspora. As a moderator for the closing reflection of the trip, I had a firsthand opportunity to see and hear how much this trip to Ghana changed their perspective on what was possible for them.

Before I left for my trip to Ghana, I talked to my dad about visiting the slave dungeons that were present in Ghana. There are not as many slave artifacts on the eastern coast of Africa (where I am from) because most of that transatlantic slave trade happened on the western coast of Africa. From my parents and extended family, I knew the extent of my Kenyan heritage, and within those stories, there was not much information about any kind of slave trade activity. I was taken aback when I talked to my dad about the trip I was going to be taking to Ghana and he shared little-known information about a slave trade that happened on the eastern coast of Africa that took Africans to Asia. He stated that it was lesser known because the enslaved were not allowed to procreate as they were transported across the Indian Ocean. This was the first time that I had been made aware that there was a slave trade that happened on the eastern coast of Africa, and I felt like there was now something missing from what I knew about my Kenyan heritage.

So as my father was helping reconcile those two stories, he reminded me that often Africans assisted slave traders to preserve their own families' lives. For those who are aware of the enslavement stories on the continent of Africa, there has always been an understanding that Africans were used to carry out the mission of the enslavers, but this was the first time that I heard how it was connected to my own family heritage. The notion that the Wangas had to participate in the enslavement efforts to save themselves and their families was devastating for me. It further impacted me when I actually went to the slave castles on the coast of Ghana and felt the everlasting atrocities perpetuated by white colonizers in a way that I became committed to figuring out how to resolve this wrongdoing before I left this earth.

As I went to different parts of the slave castle, my emotions continued to shift. In a picture, I am kneeling atop the slave dungeon, and Cadence is standing beside me. You can't tell what I was doing because of the angle of the photo, but I was crying. There's another picture where I had my hand on the wall to steady myself as I listened to the guide explain that the current height of the floor is higher than the original. Why? When the slave castle was built, the bodies of the Africans who died there were piled on top of one another as they decomposed, which heightened the level of the floor. But I also had the opportunity to spend some time with a woman who had come on the trip and had recently lost her husband unexpectedly. She traveled alone, and Cadence and I were able to spend a good part of the trip with her. In this photo, I am holding her hand as we both experienced the slave castle.

One of the first people I talked to about the trip when I returned was Brian, because while away on the trip, I knew I wanted to talk to him about whether a trip like this was something good for Target to sponsor for the Black officers the following year. When I met with Brian, we quickly determined that it was worth continuing to research and decide. After we finished that part of the conversation, we transitioned to my personal experience on the trip, because I had told him about the conversation with my dad before I departed. Brian was looking forward to hearing how it impacted my trip. After telling him the story, I told him I would figure out a way to fix this. What I was referencing was the combined set of emotions that I was processing as it related to my family's heritage and the East African slave trade. Brian's response was "I know you will." I just couldn't keep operating in that business-as-usual mode. The bag was too heavy. I felt activated for some kind of action, but I didn't know what it would be.

That conversation with Brian was probably sometime in January, right after I returned from Ghana, and that was the extent to which he and I talked about it. Three months later, when the call came in from Rich asking me to come to Essence as the CEO, I immediately called Brian, and we both knew this was it. Brian warmly said, "I'll call you this weekend." By the time Brian and I spoke next, we both knew that this was the opportunity that aligned with what I had learned about my family. Essence needed me in a very critical time for the brand, and I was being called to serve from a place of recompense based on what I had been able to achieve in corporate America and the role that Essence needed to continue to play in inspiring generations of Black girls and women and their aspirations.

# Blacktopia

The process of communicating that I was going to accept the Essence role at a critical time for Target was a change management exercise in itself. Target had not processed the idea of my leaving Target, so that ended up being what consumed a lot of Brian's and my time: communicating to the right people in the right sequence that I would be departing. Everyone from my boss, the board, the C-suite, and internal and external stakeholders would need enough information to prepare for my departure but not enough to trigger panic among the ranks. Target and Essence aligned on a communication plan that had us announcing that I would depart one month before I would actually leave Target. This would allow enough time to manage the transition of the work I would be leaving behind and offer comfort to those who were concerned about my leaving.

At the time, we did not realize that the date that we had chosen to announce I would be leaving would be the day that Target stores in Minneapolis would be getting vandalized by members of the community. The community was outraged by the murder of George Floyd that had happened a few days before. Out of an abundance of caution, we discussed if it would be the right thing to change the date of the announcement of my departure. We ultimately decided not to change the date because what was clear to us was the fact that what had become the global outcry of the murder of George Floyd was only getting started. The best thing that we could do was stick to my announcement timing. We would use the time between the date of announcing my departure and my last day at Target to create any additional resolutions necessary to manage what was happening in the Twin Cities communities.

The performance of Black talent at Target with the support of Brian and the board had been my focus for the last year. As a part of that work, I had been facilitating Brian building a relationship with the Black officers of the company, which represented the highest-ranking Black people at Target. There had been many activities that were part of building this relationship. A notable one was on a trip to Atlanta to do a market visit with the Black officers from across the company. We were looking forward to seeing one of our friends who had been promoted to officer, and he lived in Atlanta. This was our first time seeing him in person since he got promoted, and he was going to meet us at the jet terminal we would arrive at. The moment we landed and saw him, we lost it. We ran to him, hugged his neck, and loved on him the way Black folks do. We didn't care who saw or who was there. That kind of freedom and genuine expression of love and congratulations was not common for Brian to see from an officer group, and that stuck with him, and therefore a genuine kinship began.

On the morning when we announced my exit, our priority was the Black officer group. Brian broke the news, and he watched their tears of sadness and joy, because my fellow officers were happy for me but sad for Target. It had only been a week earlier when I'd called Brian the morning after George Floyd was murdered and said, "You've got to hear the way people are feeling." Brian scheduled a Zoom call with the Black officers, and he listened. He saw their tears. He felt their rage and their fear. He heard from Black men who knew him and told him that they no longer believed it was safe to come to work, not just at the store level but at corporate.

It wasn't just the high-ranking people I had put on Brian's radar; I also wanted him to connect with Black talent at other levels in the company, specifically those who had transitioned to Minneapolis just to work for Target. One of those groups was Black men who were in entry-level positions at Target headquarters. They were leaving Target at a rate of around eighteen months into their job. This was of concern, so to give Brian more context, I encouraged him to engage with them in a place where they felt the safest so that they could be fully transparent about their experiences. I said, "If you want to understand how Black men are feeling, go to them. Inviting them into your space is wonderful and carries some prestige, but to really hear them, leave your place of comfort and go to where they are comfortable: the barbershop." For those who don't know, for Black men, the barbershop is much more than a place to get a dope haircut. It's the therapist's office and the comedy shop. It's a place of healing, encouragement, and correction. It is the news, the gossip, the shared pain, and the joy. Men see one another in their truest selves. They reflect with one another, and the most powerful thing they communicate is silence when there is nothing to be said. Brian is a man, and he gets his hair cut, which is a common thread across many men. I set up a time for Brian to meet with entry-level Black men who worked at Target at a Black barber-shop. The barbershop I chose was owned by a Minneapolis native named Houston White. Many of the young men who worked at Target got their hair cut at his shop. Arranging for Brian to meet with young Black men at Houston's barbershop was a perfect way to encourage them to share their experiences candidly. Additionally, because other Black talent had moved to Minneapolis to accept positions with other corporations headquartered in Minneapolis, Houston could add context to the common threads across all the corporate Black talent who transitioned to Minneapolis. Those gatherings that we arranged had a significant impact and created several pathways that helped Black men at Target advance and stay.

Beyond the benefits that Brian got from the conversations at the barbershop that Houston referred to as "the Black Man's Country Club," the engagement that happened among Houston, the Target employees, and Brian ultimately led to Houston having several direct partnerships with Target on a clothing line, a men's body care line, and a community initiative that benefited the Camden neighbor-hood in north Minneapolis. Those partnerships continue to this day and are managed by a broader set of teams at Target that may not have been involved had we not used Houston's barbershop for the conversations between Brian and Black talent. Those things are just a few examples of just how much of my time was spent advancing Black.

I was pretty confident that because of all the activity around Brian, Houston, the Black executives at Target, and the barbershop moment, I could offer the same energy to help revive the Essence brand. Later, after I was hired at Essence, I asked Rich, "Why me?" He answered that, when he called around about me, the common thread that was shared with him was that the majority of people said that I won everywhere I went. He also added that the way that I carried myself and my passion for advancing Black were what he felt the Essence brand needed for its next era.

As I had been engaging with Essence to see opportunities for partnership with Target, my commitment to my own authenticity and my focus on Black communities were observed by a lot of the people on the Essence side, since I was partnering with them. Rich got 100 percent of Caroline, 100 percent of the time. I was just me and doing what I do, so when Rich called me about the Essence opportunity, I thought it was a joke. It was so casual that it took me a minute to understand that he was serious. I will never forget what he told me when I asked, "Why me? I am not a media person." He said, "Caroline, it's the way you live your life."

Dmitri Stockton was a Black member of the board of directors of the Target Corporation and a fellow Executive Leadership Council (ELC) member. As the news of my departure started to get around,

Dmitri called me because he was one of the board members who engaged with the Black officers frequently. Dmitri's last role had been senior vice president and special advisor to the chairman of General Electric Company. In addition to his Target board role, he served as a director to several other Fortune 500 companies. He had a particular passion for mentoring and guiding Black talent to C-suite positions and corporate boards, and I benefited a lot from his candid and direct guidance over the last few years. His call to me started with him checking in on how I was feeling. Considering we had not yet talked about the role directly, I remember responding to his question while crying and saying to him, "I know I may not be qualified for the job and I may fail, but I can't not go to serve because I am afraid to fail." His response was "I understand why you may feel that way, but I have known you for a while, and I can tell you, you're not going to fail. I am going to call you after you get started in the role, and I guarantee you that you will tell me and show me that you are not failing." As my crying got more severe from what he had said, I said, "You don't have to say that just to make me feel better." He said, "I don't give that guidance to a lot of people because I am often coaching people who don't know they may fail, and I'm trying to help them avoid the failure. So understand that I am saying this to you because I believe in you, and I wouldn't say it to you if I didn't." Dmitri kept his promise and called me a year later, and all he said was "I told you that you wouldn't fail." Since I've departed Target, he has continued to check in with me and remind me, "You are human. Stay strong and keep pushing forward. You are making a difference and are excellent in the role." One of the most frequent negative self-talk I say to myself is "I can't be the one to break Essence. This legacy, family-owned, iconic

Black cultural artifact is too critical and too sacred to not be here anymore." So, for my seven-year-old niece, Ayo, I stepped in and got to work.

What I knew about Essence before I started the role was mostly informed by what I had been told by Rich and other members of the Dennis family and what I heard from people about what they thought about Essence when I told them that I was going to work there. This information about the state of the Essence business was pretty peripheral. I knew my game plan had to start with preserving the legacy of the brand on behalf of the community it serves. One of the most fascinating perspectives I encountered when I started the role was from those who had worked in the D&I industry and now thought that my path to leading a media company was a new career path for D&I professionals. My response to them was not to consider what I had done as a new possible career path. Instead, I informed them that the path that led me to the media role I was now in was fueled by the pursuit of my purpose, not by the typical "next role" search process that most of them engaged in when they were looking for a new role. I would also share with them that the navigational guide of my purpose journey is my intuition; because of that, *I'm Highly Percent Sure* that the way I make decisions has always been about the trifecta of my gut, my heart, and my head.

When we publicly announced that I was departing Target and joining Essence, we intentionally decided that all future communications across the Essence ecosystem would begin after I started the job at Essence. I had thirty days between when we had announced my departure from Target and when I would start my job at Essence. That gave me time to focus on a successful handoff of the work that I was doing at Target to the person who would be backfilling my role.

My start date in the Essence role was June 29, 2020. At that point, we were in the early stages of the COVID pandemic, and we were just getting used to being in lockdown nationally. Also, the unrest connected to George Floyd's murder was still accelerating globally. Rich and I had decided that I would work remotely from Minneapolis for a little while, based on the assumption that the end of COVID was nearer than what we knew. The day before I was supposed to start the Essence job, a scandal about the workplace environment at Essence hit social media. The campaign targeted Essence corporate partners, entertainment partners, government partners, and the Black social media community. The advent of the scandal influenced a need for me to move to New York for my role sooner than we had initially planned, because the work that needed to be done required me to be present and in person. As you can imagine, having a humongous PR crisis the day before I was to start my new job was jarring, and there were several reach-outs to me about whether I still wanted to take the role at Essence. Considering I was supposed to start the job the next day, their inquiries were a moot point, because there was no way I was going to all of a sudden recant my acceptance of the position the day before I was supposed to start.

The experiences I was bringing with me into the Essence role had to be supplemented with subject area experts from the media world who were to be my direct reports. As the scandal unfolded, some of those impacted were the same people whom I was supposed to be working with within the role. Immediately, it was clear that I was going to be directly managing the middle layer of the organization, and my approach to doing that had to make room for what I didn't know in the industry. What took me a little bit too long to notice was the fact that my prior experiences in crisis management, workplace culture, employee relations, and external engagement were the intuitive things that I ended up having to rely on in my first three months in the role. This circumstance allowed me to flex everything I did know rather than focusing on what I didn't.

Several times as we were managing all the details that came with the need to supervise the investigations, manage internal employee sentiment, and mitigate the negative impact on our external partners, I would say to Rich, "I've done this a thousand times, but that doesn't mean I have every answer."

The investigation revealed that the accusations that were made could not be substantiated, and very quickly we had to start the work to reinvigorate the business, recover relationships, repair morale, and build the vision for the future. An example of the work we did to transform the workplace culture comes in the form of the partnership I initiated with Trudy Bourgeois, CEO of the Center for

Workforce Excellence (CWE). The result of working with CWE was a workplace culture action plan that focused on pay and performance, career and leadership development, collaboration, and cross-functional efficiency, with employees serving on a culture task force to drive the results of the plan. The totality of what I just shared pretty much consumed the remainder of the year 2020.

In 2021, as the world started to open back up, we had done the work to stabilize the operation. However, due to the limitations of COVID, I had not spent time visiting with key stakeholders because the world was in lockdown. I would consider 2021 the year that the media industry and the Essence ecosystem had an opportunity to engage with me, understand my vision for the brand, and opt in or out of the next phase of Essence.

In 2021, we embarked on a mission that included redefining the brand's reason for being, defining modernized paths for revenue, recruiting talent that had the expertise to monetize the brand's assets, and re-engaging the consumer community in making Essence Black again. Similar to the clash of workplace cultures when Essence became part of Time Inc., now there was friction between the entrepreneurial spirit of the new owner and the corporate culture that had accompanied Essence's departure from Time Warner. Moving forward, it was not just a matter of addressing the needs of employees, allocating resources, and managing the brand; there was also the added complexity of understanding and effectively managing a profit and loss (P&L) statement, a concept foreign to a group of employees that had previously operated within a large corporation and were now in a new entrepreneurial culture that would run

Essence like a small start-up. A P&L statement is a financial report that summarizes a company's revenues, expenses, and profits or losses over a specific time. It's also known as an income statement or statement of operations.

Our objective now was to set a sustainable course for growth, impact, and relevance while remaining true to the core of the Essence brand and integrating it with other brands in the portfolio. This involved strategically defining each brand, reimagining Essence Ventures, and establishing a separate P&L statement for each entity, building everything from the ground up.

In my experience spanning fifteen years at a Fortune 100 company with a market cap exceeding a hundred billion dollars and a workforce of four hundred thousand employees, I could understand the challenges faced by the Essence team that functioned under the Time Inc. ecosystem but was now transitioning into an entrepreneurial ecosystem. My coming from a company as big as Target taught me that it was everybody's obligation to function within the budget, to display fiscal discipline when it came to costs and expenses for us to meet our financial goals and receive our employee financial incentives at the end of each year. While I indirectly had financial responsibility for the P&L, my daily decisions did not impact the P&L directly. When I came into the more entrepreneurial environment of Essence Ventures in the role of president and CEO of a company much smaller than Target, it was important that I relearned the mechanics of a P&L and developed the day-to-day practice of monitoring, managing, and adjusting different parts of the P&L to ensure our organizational priorities of revenue, profit, and Earnings Before Interest, Taxes, Depreciation, and Amortization (EBITDA) were achieved. The size of the Essence Ventures business did not have a lot of cushioning to protect it if we didn't meet our revenue goals and overspent on costs. So on a daily basis I was continuing to learn from Rich the expertise tied to financial success and executive ownership of a P&L. Fiscal discipline was lacking among the four brands. All of them had been functioning on the legacy of their founder rather than determining the requirements to be competitive in the marketplace. It was up to the new owner, me, and my team to make it all happen.

Similar to Susan Taylor's surprise that Ed Lewis asked her to be the editor-in-chief, I was surprised that Rich selected me to lead the resurgence of these brands as CEO. Like Susan, I approached my role through the lens of my lived life and infused my human experience with core tenants of business as a road map for the brand's revival. The output of the road map was brand strategy, including purpose, vision, values, target audience, market analysis, awareness goals, brand personality, and voice. These activities have now led to a renewed affinity with consumers, a new reputation with partners, and a renewed position in the media industry.

The added brands that sat within Essence Ventures were strategically planned to serve the broader spectrum of Black and create new avenues for revenue. Similar to what was done in the early stages of Essence when Ed expanded to hosiery, eyewear, the Essence Awards, Essence Fest, and an Essence fashion catalogue, etc., Essence Ventures now includes four brands: Essence Communications Inc., Afropunk, BeautyCon, and Essence Studios. Essence Communications Inc. is the number one media, technology, and commerce company dedicated to Black women, with a global audience of over twenty million. Afropunk is a music festival celebrating alternative Black art, culture, and community. BeautyCon is a global platform for influential beauty, fashion, and lifestyle communities that encourages a personal definition of beauty by challenging contemporary beauty standards. Essence Studios is for the creation and distribution of original content.

What we were able to do throughout 2021 and 2022 was 100 percent revenue growth since the acquisition, 90 percent of our employees said they were proud to work at Essence, the team grew 36 percent, our average salary increased by 47 percent, and profitability grew by 260 percent. We also had record-breaking attendance and sponsorship of the Essence Festival of Culture, which included three hundred million dollars of economic impact for the city of New Orleans and the state of Louisiana. All tied to data-driven proof points that the Essence Festival of Culture is the largest festival in the country by per-day attendance.

# WangaWoman

There are a lot of benefits to the corporate structure based on its economic scale and influence. There is also a downside, which is usually focused on very little room for curated and unique experiences, especially when it comes to the people who work at the highest level of the organization. In the last few years of my Target career, my reputation as a public speaker grew very fast. With that came my first experiences with being offered payments and stipends to speak at events that I had no personal connection to. Naturally, I was excited about the opportunity to generate additional income, but those offers were in direct violation of a long-standing Target policy that Target was unable to grant me an exception on. As you can imagine, that led to a lot of frustration for me.

The Architecture of Authenticity keynote that I had become popular for was the foundation of the speaking engagement requests I would receive. So when I transitioned to Essence and began working for a family that was entrepreneurial and innovative about how to create multiple sources of income, it gave me the freedom to accept the offers for paid speaking engagements.

While I was excited about the opportunity to accept these offers, I miscalculated how overwhelming managing those requests was going to be operationally and economically. To get a handle on it all, I asked my daughter to help me get things organized. She ended up cofounding the business WangaWoman with me, specifically handling the incoming requests, preparing for the ones accepted, and completing each engagement financially. As Cadence and I did that work, we got to a point where we figured we should go legit, but we had no idea where to start. Case in point, in the beginning, we used Cash App to receive payments. La Juana Whitmore and I had worked together at Target, where she was the lead enterprise business architect. Over time at Target, we had conversations about the Black talent experience, what it was, and, more importantly, what it needed to be, and ultimately, when she decided to leave Target to start a consulting firm for small business owners, I could be nothing but happy for her. So, a few years later, when Cadence and I needed help figuring out how to formalize our business, we reached out to La Juana to see if she could help. Not only was La Juana the perfect person to help us with what we needed, it serendipitously became a family affair. WangaWoman LLC was officially registered in October 2020 and was started by me; my daughter, Cadence; La Juana Whitmore; her daughter Ra Janae (RJ); and her granddaughter Camilah. Every Saturday, for four hours, the five of us, who were in four different time zones, would meet and do WangaWoman business. Although we are not all still involved in the same way, we still use Saturday mornings to get our business done.

One of the funniest things about those interactions was the many moments of mothers against daughters, frequently tied to current events and/or culture. This ultimately meant we only did business for about three hours, because the first hour was always dedicated to the battle of the Gen Xers versus the millennials, with Camilah being the only thing we were all aligned on. Here were two mothers and their older daughters meeting every Saturday for four hours, hashing out ideas, beginning to lay the foundation for a company, and taking care of the business side of a business. What sticks out in my mind are the beautiful "us" and "them" components we shared. La Juana and I would toss an idea in, and Cadence and RJ would look at each other like, "Um, no." The same thing would happen the other way around. It was fun. We didn't plan it that way, but it worked so well. Because the spectrum of the generations represented by the four of us provided richness and informed the way we thought about the business. Without those varied perspectives, there would have been gaps. One of my favorite parts of this partnership was that both Cadence and RJ had creative interests. It was fun to see them have the opportunity to apply that creativity in different ways, including being approached by Bounce TV to produce a segment for the Trumpet Awards.

WangaWoman's fourth quarter in 2020 was focused on strategic planning, which produced things like WangaWoman's vision, mission, values, financial goals, operational structure, and administrative support. The year 2021 was all about further defining the brand, which included building an intake process, getting legit, templating, operationalizing our products, finalizing our visual identity as a brand, and accepting and processing incoming requests. We ultimately decided that our mission was to democratize authenticity by connecting people and places to the purpose they needed to fulfill in the world. Considering that authenticity had become a buzzword with no real meaning, it was important for us to be clear about what we meant by it. That is what led to the development of an "authenticity maturity framework." This was a set of criteria we used to assess where a company's authenticity maturity was and connect it to the right resources within our portfolio.

The framework has four stages that are pretty easy to comprehend. What differentiates our approach is the added fifth stage. Beyond the fourth stage, where the focus is primarily on you, the fifth stage is altruistic and highlights each of our accountability to build others up, even when there is nothing in it for you. It is to hold people accountable for equipping those around them with the tools that lead to their success, with a focus on accelerating how those behind you get to their purpose faster by not making the same mistakes that you made. It is the difference between being noticed (stage four) and being known (stage five). It focuses on a legacy rather than an achievement. It is the only way we will continue to drive progress between generations. Without it, the work an individual does to find their authenticity dies when they do.

As we continued to develop the business, each of our individual skill sets and experiences manifested in different ways and ultimately delayed the realization that we needed marketing support for the brand. So we put together a request for proposal (RFP), submitted that RFP, and screened possible marketing agencies to help build our brand. We would find something we liked in the various candidates, but we always felt something was missing when it came to how they translated who we were into a marketing approach. As we contemplated what to do about this somehow, we remembered that Cadence does graphic design. Cadence submitted a total and complete brand-and-style guide that she just did on the side, because she was looking to be more creative compared to what she did for her day job. One day, Cadence shared it with us, and we realized that Cadence had created most of what we were trying to get marketing agencies to do for us. It included a logo, a color scheme, and multiple graphic ways that our brand could be displayed on merchandise. In true typical Cadence fashion, when we started to hype her up based on what she had delivered to us, she made us the problem, because she doesn't like anyone bringing attention to her work and skills. But her mama (me) and La Juana overrode all the noise she was making and implemented pretty much everything she had created, which eliminated any need to engage outside marketing support. The theme related to how much the ethos of WangaWoman was and has continued to be self-explanatory, self-sufficient, and self-reliant on the skills of the core team and word-of-mouth recommendations from the communities we serve. This is further proven by a 600 percent increase in revenue since 2020.

While we anticipated that the majority of our revenue would come from speaking engagements and organizations, our business model expanded to include consumer-focused products, including self-paced courses, merchandise, and affiliate marketing. Toward the end of 2021, consulting with businesses became less and less interesting to me. But what did stick was the outgrowth of invitations to conferences. At the beginning of 2022, we launched courses that clients could access on their own through the website and never attend a conference. The courses spawned the monthly Coffee with

Caroline, where I videoconference with anyone who has purchased a course to answer questions, shoot the shit, or just listen. At the beginning of 2023, as the business started to grow, Cadence took a step back from the operations role, and RJ left to go to dentistry school. I knew I couldn't run WangaWoman and Essence simultaneously, so La Juana was the perfect choice to take over as CEO.

WangaWoman has expanded from its primary function as a hub for my speaking engagements to classes, online courses, curricula, and creative agency. But no matter what we offer virtually, folks still want to hear and see me in person. Which still blows my mind. One of the things that has always fascinated me in my career is how people react to the way I communicate. Sometimes it is them responding to me as "eloquent" or "articulate"; other times it is my being asked how I learned to communicate this way. One time I was even asked if I learned it at Toastmasters. Contrary to popular belief, I have never taken a course or participated in any sort of training or coaching related to speaking publicly. Most people can't believe that during a speech, I am thinking about what I'm going to say next while I'm speaking, which means I also don't use notes, note cards, a teleprompter, an outline, a script, or any other sort of guided speaking tool. My process is pretty organic. Sometimes I can visualize the sequence of what I want to share. Other times I just follow where the story I'm telling takes me. But most of the time, I forget what I've said as soon as I say it, because I tend to be able to say the same things many different ways and often forget the way I said it right after I've said it. In working with teams and communication professionals, I have always advised that they turn on some kind of recording device to record what I share when they come to seek my perspective. What that helps with is a documented recollection of what I have just said, as well as mitigating words getting lost, as I talk fast. Transitioning to the public stage as a speaker was not difficult for me, because I approached a big audience the same way I approached a one-on-one conversation.

One of the things that I have a reputation for is telling simple stories with humor and connection to take the audience to the learning objective I am trying to drive. You can call it something I was just gifted with and have been able to leverage throughout my career. But it is even more prominent based on what I do within WangaWoman and with my Essence Ventures role, where I am often required to engage with big audiences. As you have read me write before in other chapters, it is extremely important to me that I tell the full story of my experiences. Not just the triumphs but the trials as well, which ensures that the audience hears the story as it actually happened as I was in it instead of a sanitized version based on how I want it to be remembered. I decided that this would be important because of the experiences I had listening to inspirational leaders, who told perfect stories that caused me to believe that I could not achieve their level of success because I knew how imperfect I was.

What continues to be the most valuable part of what we offer at WangaWoman is the in-person delivery—defined by what I just shared as my approach to public speaking and the perspective that I offer—it is real-ass storytelling, and does not necessarily change based on platform (i.e., a stage, a book, a show, a course, etc.). Rest assured that the evolution of WangaWoman will continue to have those things at its core.

# Mind Ya Business

I had a *Back to the Future* moment in 2023 with the creation and release of the *Time of Essence* documentary. There was so much that I came to understand differently about the legacy and logistics of Essence. While helpful, it was nonetheless a kind of after-the-fact moment, since by the time the documentary was filmed, I was already CEO of the company. This is no commercial for the doc, but if you haven't seen *Time of Essence*, the five-part documentary about the fifty-year history of Essence, you should check it out.

The series is inspiring, messy, encouraging, challenging, and a call to action. The documentary is a tribute to the enduring spirit of Essence. It highlights themes that have been the brand's cornerstone: the significance of community and the collective voice, the importance of resilience and the ability to thrive against the odds, and the unwavering commitment to authenticity and purpose. These are the pillars that not only supported Essence's past but also continue to guide its future. Watching *Time of Essence* is like participating in an ongoing dialogue about the contributions and triumphs of the Black community.

After Rich and I participated in our portion of the documentary, the documentary producers asked me to come back and do the voice-over narration for the entire series. It was educational and blew my fucking mind to understand how much history repeats itself. I didn't even know what I was going to say. I had zero prep. I learned things about this company called Essence that I was now running while I was reading the copy (narrating script). With all that I was processing as we were creating the documentary, there were a few themes across the then and the now that stuck out to me, and I would love to share a few of those.

## Not an *Essence* Woman

When it came to tackling the tough issues that faced Black folks, Susan L. Taylor, former editor-in-chief of *Essence* magazine, was fearless. When a story came her way that she knew merited the attention of *Essence*, she had no qualms about doing what needed to be done. So when Isis Sapp-Grant approached *Essence* to tell her story, Susan listened. Isis was no joke. She was a young girl and a gang member in New York whose story needed to be heard. In the *Time of Essence* documentary, she talks about how it was so bad that, at seventeen years old, she kept a dark outfit ready to go, because she knew somebody was going to die. It was crazy; it seemed like she was going to a funeral every week. But here's the thing: Isis didn't grow up poor and underprivileged. She was just lost and trying to survive the streets, so she chose to become a teenage gangbanger. It was about survival. Nobody was safe, but it was mostly about belonging and power.

Isis was the queen until she got popped for robbery. When her mother saw her shackled, it broke her heart. Isis said her mother was like, "I never thought I'd see this day come. Not my child. We come from people who were put in chains, and they didn't have a choice, and here you are choosing chains!" Seeing the pain on her mother's face broke something in Isis. That moment changed everything for her. She wanted out. But it ain't that easy to get out. To get out of the Decepticons, Isis hit up teachers, her parents, and even a cop who was king to her to get out of the street gang she had founded. They agreed that she should go away to college.

She got her BA from the State University of New York at Stony Brook (SUNY) and her Master of Social Work (MSW) from New York University (NYU). Afterward, she started doing one-on-one therapy with kids at risk for involvement in gangs, leading workshops in schools, and traveling the subways and talking to the kids there. A whole new generation of Decepts (slang for "Decepticons") is out there now, as well as other groups, like the Latin Kings, the Crips, and the Bloods. When she reached out to *Essence*, she had already formed Blossom, the first community-based diversion and alternative to incarceration program specifically designed for Black girls, other girls of color, and LGBTQ+ youth.

Why am I telling you all this? As inspirational as this story is, when Susan decided to make Isis's story, called "Gang Girl," the cover of the August 1998 issue, *Essence* readers were very loud about the fact that this type of woman did not belong on the cover of *Essence*.

A reader wrote, "How dare you put a gangbanger (former or not) on the cover of *Essence* magazine. *Essence* isn't just a magazine; it is an institution. Did you hear what she said she did? How could you, *Essence*?"

For the January/February 2023 issue of *Essence*, we decided to have Lori Harvey, model, socialite, and business owner, on the cover of the Black love issue. She was selected because of the way she navigates modern-day dating by deciding to start or stop relationships based on what makes her happy. This is actually a form of self-love, but this way of moving about and around the dating scene has become something that people have used to judge her. She does not often do interviews, so we were excited about being able to carry her first-person voice. It was important for us to highlight her most candid and authentic thoughts for the reader. Similar to what took place with Isis, the *Essence* community had a lot to say about the decision to put Lori on the cover. A lot of their narrative was tied to her not being an *Essence* woman.

"Wow, *Essence*."

"Not attacking her personally . . . but why? Truly not understanding the decision-making nor the vision of *Essence* anymore."

"How could you? She is not an *Essence* woman!"

In both of these scenarios, the community tried to dictate what an Essence woman was, and the brand had a responsibility to represent the spectrum of what being a Black woman is in society.

## Audacious Acceptance

As the *Time of Essence* documentary covered the nineties, it delved into the story of Linda Villarosa, *Essence*'s health editor, and how she revealed to Susan Taylor that she was a lesbian. The flood of compassion that she got back from Susan gave her the courage to not only come out to the rest of her co-workers but also led to having her and her mother featured in the Mother's Day issue. Linda and her mom, Clara, cowrote a powerful piece that touched on the unspoken but understood homophobia in the Black community. It wasn't just significant that Linda told her story; it was the fact that her mother was a part of it that challenged generational perspectives on homosexuality.

I attended my first Essence Black Women in Hollywood event in 2019. I remember being moved by Niecy Nash's remarks, one of that year's honorees. She had recently gone public with her divorce. When she took the stage to accept her award, she became overwhelmed with tears; it was clear that she was going through something. You could tell this was bigger than the award itself. She thanked Essence for giving her the space to share her pain. It wasn't until later that she came out and introduced the world to Jessica, her partner.

When we chose to feature Niecy and her wife on the April 2022 cover of the magazine, I was surprised to learn that this would be the first time that *Essence* had a same-sex couple on the magazine cover. Considering the journey since Linda and her mother's courageous story, one would have expected that *Essence* would have addressed this issue earlier than 2022. This moment highlighted how much work we still needed to do to give equitable acceptance to the LGBTQ+ community within the Black community.

I was proud of our decision to feature Niecy and her wife on the cover, as it compelled our community to confront a matter that had been ignored. The acquisition of Afropunk into the Essence Ventures portfolio allowed us to give direct attention to the parts of the Black community that have been pushed to the margins because what they represent does not match what the Black community will accept. In 2023, we embedded Afropunk Blacktopia into the Essence Festival of Culture to assist our many Black subcommunities with coexisting healthily. By no means are we where we need to be. Whether it's Linda's story or Niecy's story, there are still very few places where our community has reconciled equal existence for members of the LGBTQ+ community who just happen to be Black. Essence will continue to use its voice to drive change and hold our community accountable for healing this wound.

## Family Business

Family can be defined in a lot of ways. There is your born family and your chosen family. When we look at how Essence was founded, we see that it was founded by what I call a chosen family. In 1970, four Black men—Ed Lewis, Cecil Hollingsworth, Clarence Smith, and Jonathan Blount—had an idea for a magazine about and for Black women. In the very same way that a traditional family shares values, money, and space, this chosen family of Black men functioned as a family in the context of business on behalf of a critical member of the human community: the Black woman.

During that era, it was highly unlikely that a Black woman would have been allowed to start a magazine for Black women. Recognizing their gender privilege, a group of Black men took the initiative to create something that became bigger than they probably ever imagined it would be when they started it. Just like any other family business, things started with everyone coming to a place of agreement, but the more things changed, the more they disagreed.

So let's start with what the documentary tells us about the money. Freedom National Bank, which was founded by Jackie Robinson, loaned them thirteen thousand dollars as seed money. They increased their credibility and ability to get more funding by pursuing acclaimed director and fashion photographer Gordon Parks. With Gordon on board, they received more attention, and Ed was able to travel to Chicago to meet with Hugh Hefner, founder of Playboy Enterprises, Inc., and ultimately, Ed secured

$250,000 from him. However, as financial success followed, new challenges emerged within the family-like dynamic of Essence. More money, more problems!

Gordon Parks left because he did not like the creative direction; Ed had been appointed CEO and had conflicts with Jonathan Blount, so he fired him; and Cecil was dismissed due to concerns about his conduct. As a result of all these departures, a takeover was being planned by some of the partners who had left the business. All the activity tied to the takeover was extremely disruptive to the operations of the business internally. The employees were shareholders, and they had to decide if they were going to allocate their shares to the group vying to take over the company or stick with Ed. After the takeover attempt failed, Essence's financial success accelerated.

The magazine was doing well, so Ed made attempts to acquire other media entities. During that process, Ed received an offer from Time Inc. to buy Essence. Just like in any other family, there was concern from the employees, subscribers, readers, and the media that by selling Essence to Time, Essence would lose its focus on Black woman. However, the sale was completed. In the face of certain concerns and uncertainties, Susan L. Taylor remained with the company during the transitional period. However, as Time Inc. gradually diluted the Black focus of the Essence brand, it led to the fragmentation of the Essence ecosystem and family. For nearly two decades, these estranged family groups disconnected from Essence, and as a result, the business suffered.

The financial underperformance of Essence was so bad that when Time Inc. was sold to another company, they did not want Essence, so Essence was not included in the sale. Similar to Essence's founding, it took a Black man with some money to prevent

*Essence*'s demise by purchasing *Essence* from Time Inc. so it would not be defunct. This turn of events mirrored the challenges faced during *Essence*'s founding. With that purchase, the new family that is now running *Essence* was not a chosen family; it was a born family, the Dennis family, led by Richelieu Dennis. Ironically, the same exercises that happened in *Essence*'s founding had to happen again.

## Love Letters/People Are Talking

One of the things Susan was focused on during her tenure as editor-in-chief was understanding how the community was thinking and feeling. She did this in several ways, including flying around the country and having focus groups with different groups of women to hear what was on their minds. At other times it was responding to something that had happened in society that they were talking about. One of those moments was the story of Vanessa Williams.

When Vanessa Williams was crowned Miss America in 1984, it was a big moment for Black women around the world, and Essence participated in celebrating that historic moment. Anytime a Black woman makes history, there is always some kind of covert retaliation from whatever establishment she is breaking into. When Vanessa ended up in a scandal tied to some controversial photos she had taken before she had become Miss America, there were calls for her to resign from her reign as Miss America. Although Vanessa ended up giving up her crown as a result of the scandal, *Essence* still had an obligation to engage with the community as they processed the situation. One of those things was tied to the cover of an edition of the magazine that featured Vanessa's moment, which had already gone to print at the point that her scandal hit and she resigned. There was pressure from advertisers not to run that edition of the magazine because of concerns of what the scandal would do to their corporate reputations. *Essence* decided to run it anyway despite the risk and stand with her. The other way in which *Essence* responded to the moment was Susan dedicating one of her "In the Spirit" columns to Vanessa. It was essentially a call to grace for Black folks and a love letter to Vanessa. The hard copy flew off the stands, but the magazine lost subscribers and sponsors. But here's the thing: *Essence* put their arms around Vanessa and supported her. That's who they were, and that's who we still are.

Modern-day *Essence* continues to monitor the existence of Black women in society similar to what was done when the magazine was founded. With new tools and technology, we become informed faster and can respond faster in the digital age. Our version of Susan's "In the Spirit" column is, when a Black woman is being maligned in public, we post love letters on our social media platforms to uplift her in solidarity with our community. Social media is also the platform that we use to listen in real time to what is on the hearts and minds of the Black women we serve. Our social media posts, comments, and environments continue to be the place where Black women come to when they need rest, recognition, or recompense.

So when Sara Sidner, a Black anchor on CNN, made an announcement that she had stage three breast cancer, we wrote a love letter to Sara on our Instagram page.

It read:

*Vulnerability. Strength. Compassion. Fortitude. These aren't just words, these are the core characteristics of Sara Sidner.*

*Thank you for sharing your journey with Breast Cancer with the world. Through your voice, many will be helped.*

*Through your bravery, many lives will be saved. You've been an advocate for women all over the world, and now it's time that we return that support to you.*

*Sara sends this reminder, "To all my sisters, Black and white and brown out there, please, for the love of God, get your mammograms every single year. Do your self-exams. Try to catch it before I did."*

*If you will, the good book says, "Be strong and courageous. Do not be afraid; do not be discouraged, for the Lord your God will be with you wherever you go." We, your ESSENCE family, will be there every step of the way!*

This was Sara's reply:

*bless you @essence for all you do to make us feel like queens. We deserve better from our medical system. we must demand better. Having met the head of this company [Caroline Wanga] I can tell you there is NO ONE more fierce than she. not a single human*

# Nudges

Consider this a brief break, a teaching moment, or just a few things I want to spend a bit more time talking about: introversion and my self-compassion plan.

People always struggle to accept that I am an introvert because they react to my personality. They see humor, charisma, and word-play, which contradict their assumptions that all introverts are shy, demure, and quiet people. My introversion dictates how much energy I have for interaction with other people. I call it my social battery. I have to constantly pay attention to how much human interaction is scheduled or possible for me on any given day in any given role. That assessment ensures that I can store up as much energy as needed in advance, arrange how to manage my energy in the moment, or devise a plan for how to recover energy after the fact. No matter which plan I choose, the fact remains that without planning, my energy will be drained, and at that point, I am unable to function in a healthy manner, so I just check out, whether I want

## AN INTROVERT

I AM... I LIKE BEING ALONE... A LOT.

to or not. It has become even more important as I have continued to have roles that require a lot of human interaction on a regular basis, which significantly impacts how well I perform in each role. Knowing that has helped me advocate fiercely for my needs, particularly since my career requires me to navigate spaces filled with public interaction that require me to be "on."

Frequently, people express surprise when they learn about my introversion, because they already have an idea of who they think I am and are locked into a stereotypical image of what an introvert should look like. Even those who follow me have a hard time reconciling my online persona with my introverted nature, yet social media is one of the ways that I manage to balance my energy, since it allows me to engage with people without having to manage the response immediately. When I combine my clinical depression, my introversion, the physical manifestation of my type-two diabetes, and high-stress jobs, the need to have an active plan and approach to energy management is of highest criticality. The reason for this nudge is for those who might have some or all of what I have just listed; it is important that you know that it should not be an automatic assumption that you cannot be successful in roles like mine with factors like these.

The most important tool in my tool kit that helps me be successful is my self-compassion plan. I've learned to give myself grace and allow for rest when I need it. This can mean taking time for myself in my hotel room or finding a quiet corner and simply being still for a while; it can mean delegating a role to someone on my team or renegotiating a format for human interaction. Self-care is vital to my work and one of the main reasons I can do what I do. I want to show that you don't have to be an extrovert to be successful. You just need to be strategic about looking after yourself. It's all about balance and making space for what you need. I don't have to pretend to be someone I'm not, and neither do you!

I grew up in corporate America, and during that time, I underwent every imaginable psychological assessment—most notably the Myers-Briggs Type Indicator (MBTI). This tool doesn't just lend insights; it evaluates where you stand on the continuum between introversion and extroversion. With each trait maxing out at thirty points on this scale, I'm an introvert's introvert, having hit the ceiling with a score of thirty. Until those assessments in the corporate sphere were revealed to me, I was struggling with not being an extrovert and pretended to be one because it was more socially acceptable.

Consequences for forcing myself to pretend to be an extrovert included accepting guilt when people told me that I was "anti-social" or flaky because I was always ready to leave an event early, I would try to negotiate not going at all, or I would cancel at the last minute. The confusing and hurtful part was that they weren't wrong about the behavior, but none of us understood why those behaviors happened, so I just accepted what people told me was the reason why. Once I understood introversion, I realized that being an introvert is not a cookie-cutter type of situation; several attributes can characterize introversion. For example, there's this misconception that all introverts are reserved or have quiet voices, and all extroverts are loud. Not true. These characteristics are not the standard for everyone. What dawned on me was that my introverted nature is deeply connected to my "social battery," and the speed of its depletion is simply how it manifests in me. Reflecting on my past, I see why people perceived me as always looking for an out. The truth is, my readiness to retreat or isolate predominantly hinged on whether my social battery was charged. In learning more about myself, it became evident that I cannot dictate when my social battery drains, but what I can master is how to replenish it, particularly when I am due to invest a significant amount of social energy.

The Essence Black Women in Hollywood weekend is a good example. It requires substantial social interaction with celebrities and the who's who of Hollywood, which many people would consider to be exciting and most people look forward to. "Exciting" and "something I look forward to" are accurate, because I am passionate about highlighting those who are doing great work within entertainment culture. To prepare for that event, I tried to spend as many consecutive hours as possible alone before the event to store up the maximum amount of energy needed to successfully survive that event. This is not just important for me; it is even more critical for those who participate in the event, those who are honored as a part of the event, and those who watch the event. Those in attendance could misinterpret a difference in my energy as a lack of importance, significance, and celebration of the accomplishments of those highlighted. Learning to do this helped me articulate who I am with others and balance my roles in work, personal relationships, and beyond while making others feel acknowledged and still safeguarding my well-being.

I mentioned depression a bit earlier. Let me tell you what happened during my journey regarding depression. One afternoon I was on an ordinary drive home from work—not an especially terrible day or anything. I started crying uncontrollably, to the point where I could not see the road I was driving on, I was struggling to breathe, and I was disoriented—all while driving over sixty miles an hour on the highway in pouring rain. I knew I could not continue to drive since I could not see the road, and I was worried that I was going to cause an accident. So all I tried to do was pull over. Once I pulled over, I did not know what was wrong, but I did know that I was not okay. All that I could think of was to call Cara McNulty, who was a behavioral health expert on the Target Benefits

Team, which I had been working with on some of our mental health awareness programing. While I would now call her a close friend, at the time, she came to the forefront of my mind for a reason I don't understand, but she saved my life. When I called her, I told her I needed to go to the psych ward, because that was all I could think of. Based on her expertise, she did her own assessment, understood what I was dealing with, and didn't bother with explaining it to me; she focused on helping me get home safely.

The very next day, she coordinated with Target's on-site physician, who was also my primary doctor, Dr. Rierson, to organize a leave of absence. Dr. Rierson then connected me to a few program options that would help me work through the moment. I ended up participating in a thirty-day outpatient program at Fairview Riverside Hospital (the same hospital where Cadence was born) focused on mental health and illness. Now, at this point, "depression" wasn't a term they were using with me yet. I was numb at this point, and since I had entered the program, I figured why I was numb would be made clear during the program. So, through the program, I learned that depression was what I was dealing with, what things triggered it, how it worked, what it was, how it impacted a person, and how to live with it.

The program included both one-on-one components with psychiatrists, therapists, and wellness experts and group sessions with other patients in the program with similar diagnoses and lived experiences. For about a month, a dozen or so of us shared our stories and experiences with one another to support one another's growth and learning in support of living with a better relationship with mental health.

After thirty days in the program, I returned to work at Target. Brian had life experience helping and supporting people with mental health issues and called me into his office on my first day back. I could tell from the way he was looking at me that he did not feel that I was as well as I thought I was, so he encouraged me to take more time off. No matter how hard he tried to convince me that I wasn't ready to return, I insisted that I was. Lo and behold, he was right, because later that day, in the middle of an unrelated corporate workshop about energy management (yeah—the irony is not lost on me), I had an overly emotional response to a benign question the program facilitator asked. All my colleagues in the class definitely looked surprised, because they knew that was not who I usually was. After seeing their faces, I accepted that I probably needed a little more time away from work.

I really thought that completing the thirty-day program was enough for me to return to work. What I did not realize was that the program taught me what depression was and how to manage it, but I had yet to actually put it into practice in real life. So I took another thirty-day leave, and this time I just stayed at home and began working on all the tools I had been given and how to fit them into my everyday life. It was just me at home, and I didn't know how to be with "me" in a healthy way. Of all the tools I was given, the one of highest value, then and now, is my self-compassion plan. While it was a requirement for release from the first thirty-day program, it became the rhythm of my day, when all I had was the day and figuring out what to do in that day.

After that second set of thirty days, I returned to Target equipped with knowing how I needed support from those I worked with to stay healthy in my role. This time when Brian saw me after my return, he looked at me and just said, "Now you are ready." The hardest part of garnering the support I needed at work was telling my boss, my peers, my team, and my partners that I needed their help in adhering to the commitments on my self-compassion plan, because if they did not help me do it, I was not going to be able to do it for myself. As much as I was worried about judgment from them, their response was filled with love, care, and commitment to help me be well. To this day, that's the only way that I can stay healthy. That's how my self-compassion plan came to be. To understand more about how this plan came to life and still helps me to this day, take a look at my self-compassion plan course, which you can access here.

While my self-compassion plan came with my battle with depression, it served my introverted side too. In the same way that reducing social interactions helps with navigating through dark moments, my self-compassion plan equally applies when I experience social exhaustion. The plan supports balance, regardless of whether it stems from low energy or heavy depression states, because they mimic each other's role in creating isolation so I can restore energy and regain focus.

# Denga

I'm a person who always tries to give people and situations nicknames just for the fun of it. Rich's last name is Dennis, my last name is Wanga, so for shits and giggles, we shall be referred to as "Denga."

One of the things that continues to be fascinating to me is that although Rich and I have only known each other since 2019, the way we think, the way we want to impact the world, and our belief in what often looks impossible are synced as if we have known each other our whole lives. Whenever Rich and I are presenting or discussing the Essence Ventures business with an audience, it is often referred to as "the Rich-Caroline experience." Our hectic schedules don't always allow us to be in the same room at the same time, but when we do get in the same room, we vibe seamlessly. One of the things that Rich has always said to me since I have worked for him is that one of the things that he is best at is building great teams. He has an eye for talent and people before they can see it in themselves. He also has a high risk tolerance, which allows him to have patience to fill in the competence gaps that people have yet to overcome. The people Rich brings on to his teams experience his generosity and his very loud loyalty to the extent that they basically feel like they are members of his family.

So now you may be able to better understand what was in his head when he picked me. Because technically, I was not qualified for the job. He often reminds me that the way I live out my authenticity and the fact that I win everywhere that I go are what he wanted in the next person to lead the Essence brand. What I didn't know about media or had not done before as it related to the job of CEO, he would assist by supplementing any deficiencies with the hiring of people with expertise in those areas to help coach and teach me the media business. In turn, he assigned responsibilities based on actual competencies. When it came to expertise in the media business, we prioritized hiring brand leadership roles with technical expertise and seasoned tenure to surround my role with talent who knew the industry. Because of my own learning style and Rich's immersive teaching style, there have been real-time shadowing, in-depth working sessions, external benchmarking, and network introductions that have accelerated my level of knowledge of the media industry. That included a room like the Ad Council dinner, which is an advertising philanthropic event with the who's who of the media industry. It included a one-on-one dinner he hosted with the CEO of a company we were considering entering into a partnership with, and it included co-presenting with him to a group of marketing professionals to get them to invest in Essence Ventures. He often says when we are in a room together, "I will never speak after Caroline," because one of the things he appreciates in me is my ability to inspire people to join us on our mission, to align with the value of what our brand offers. The phenomenal business results we have been able to drive over the last few years have been achieved successfully because of his investment in making sure I understand how we win in the marketplace.

There is one place where Rich and I could not be further apart: Rich is an extrovert . . . extrovert! He doesn't need very many hours of sleep, he loves to entertain, he is extremely generous, and he has a big heart. While we are aligned on having a big heart, I am undeniably an introvert whose social battery drains fast when there has to be a lot of human interaction at the same time. In the circumstance of this job, that could be a deal-breaker; thankfully, Rich and I have found a rhythm that allows my introversion to be present but still meet the core expectations of my role. An example of this is when I greet everyone when I arrive at a large gathering, but I depart discreetly because I'm usually leaving long before the event is scheduled to end. But when I do say goodbye to people when I'm leaving, they try to get me to stay. Hence why I'm known for my poofin'. I will poof on your ass in a minute; if you have not experienced it from me, you will. In true Rich fashion, he has accepted how my introverted behavior shows up, but he never lets a moment pass by without making fun of me for it. Anytime he sees me trying to leave, he will get the attention of everybody gathered and state, "Hey, everybody. Caroline is sick of people and is leaving." Those petty moments bring him so much joy, so I deal with them.

The Rich and Caroline Dynamic:

- **Preferably Petty:** We lean into our petty disagreements with a touch of humor, knowing that the slightest provocations are merely an entertaining sideshow to our grand camaraderie.

- **Heavily Jovial:** Our interactions are drenched in laughter and mirth, the kind of rich, booming joy that reverberates through walls and warms the spirits of those around us.

- **Big Visionaries:** Together, we dream in broad strokes, creating expansive panoramas of what can be. We aspire to loftier realities, unbound by the limits of what is deemed possible.

- **Selectively Optimistic:** Our outlook is cautiously hopeful. We choose our moments of optimism, injecting it where we believe it can flourish and mitigating its presence where we sense disappointment may lurk.

- **Calm Chaos:** Even amidst disorder and frenetic energy, we find a serene steadiness. It's an ordered disarray where we find both comfort and clarity.

- **Blackity Black:** In every facet, we embody the culture. We are unapologetically Black, and we stand in its legacy, intricacies, and resilience in every aspect of who we are and what we do.

- **All About the Money:** Our dynamic is fueled by an unyielding pursuit of financial success. Every move is calculated toward wealth accumulation for us and those tethered to our circle.

- **Work Hard to Play Hard:** We are relentless in our labor—a formidable hustle drives us. Yet that same intensity fuels our recreation; the harder we work, the grander the celebration.

- **Complete Opposites:** Like two divergent halves of a whole, we sit at polar ends of a spectrum. This contrast adds depth to our alliance, as complementing contrasts often do.

- **Melded Minds:** Despite our differences—or perhaps because of them—our intellects have fused. There lies a synergy in our thoughts, an interlocking of ideas that creates a robust foundation for innovation and creativity.

Rich fits into that small group of entrepreneurs who change history. I underestimated how much I would value being in proximity to him as the optimist, the visionary, the disrupter, the entertainer, the giver, the teacher, the hype man, the funmaker, and—a little-known fact—the master gardener, as the garden is where he does all his "world domination" thinking. I now present Rich Dennis.

My first meeting with Caroline was confirmation to me that unicorns do exist. As it turns out, she was the best choice and a perfect fit for the job as CEO of Essence Ventures. A quick note to leaders who are evaluating talent: As far back as I can remember, even as a kid, I've been very competitive, and I always want to be around the best. I look for that same insatiable drive and competitive nature in other people. I know that somebody who has those types of characteristics is going to be an incredible leader, operator, or parent. But those characteristics, alone and without the smarts—meaning the ability to process and sort through issues—will materialize as just exerted energy. The combination of smarts, the idea of wanting to be the best, the curiosity to learn how to be the best, and the desire to invest in yourself are all good indicators of future success.

My intuition is often influenced by my experiences. Inevitably, intuition works to help you amplify the discernment around who someone is, and it helps to reveal the things that are not immediately obvious. So the more that you work on your intuition, the sharper it becomes. You begin to recognize quicker what is going to work and what is not going to work. This rapidly grows from being an intuition to being a way of thinking. I may have a particular feeling about someone by just being around them. I may get stimuli from listening to them talk. But very quickly, it turns into sort of a scientific analysis of what works and what does not work. What is going to be of value, and what is not going to be of value? I think intuition is what creates the opportunity to receive. But then you need those other elements very quickly to help process it.

Caroline and I care about the same things; we care about our community, we care about our teams, and we care about our people in a real way. I say this because I think people mistake caring for something or someone as patting people on the back and giving them awards or giving them recognition. I'm not saying not to do those things. But caring is also helping people make hard choices, helping them recognize where they can be better. And that is probably more valuable to somebody than just helping them develop what they are great at.

Caroline and I have very different styles; we have very different personalities. Caroline fills a room when she walks in. You wouldn't notice if I was in a room. I guess I would say she's a big personality. If you didn't know who I was, you wouldn't know that I was there. With Caroline, you don't have to know who she is to know that she's there. We are different in several ways, but we both care about solving the same problems. That is where we are perpetually aligned. We're focused on solving the same issues, which is a quite powerful thing. It just goes to show you that it doesn't take one kind of personality or one kind of thought process to work toward amazing outcomes.

I am very big on unification. The unification of our culture. The coming together of Black people globally—if not physically, at least intellectually. I dream that we will understand our various cultures and embrace them and one another. I believe economic inclusion is a human right. I think separating Black people across the planet, across the globe, all these centuries has inhibited our ability to be included in these various economies fairly and equitably. As a result, we get very small pieces of the economic opportunity pie. This has also separated us culturally. Therefore, rather than absorbing our vast cultures, we tend to use those cultures as separators. That is how we were separated from one another historically.

The diversity and the beauty of our respective cultures were weaponized into true weapons of mass division (WMDs). We see a future of bringing Black people together, whether they were born in Zambia, Senegal, Addis Ababa, or in Chicago, New York, Los Angeles, or Alabama. Consider the power of what could happen if we had a collective thought about how we drive economics in our communities. It could become an extraordinarily powerful equalizer around economic inclusion and equity. There is a real conversation about ways to create every opportunity for every Black person equally. We want to see the Black community globally have an opportunity to grow. One of the best ways to grow is to understand, recognize, appreciate, and partner with one another to drive that growth, no matter where we come from. No matter where we happen to be born.

Media is the medium through which we can connect our cultures, where people can explore our different cultures, where people can engage with one another, where people can exchange ideas, whether they agree, but at least they can exchange and they can have viewpoints shared. Media is also a platform to educate. It is a place where we can educate the quickest, and the most efficiently on who we are and what we are, as well as our differences and our similarities. In media, we get to share thoughts and ideas, which come in the form of art, in the form of words, and in the form of physical expression. Having this platform allows us to do just that. The more of these platforms that we have that don't just speak to the Black community but speak to the broader community, the more we can demystify who we are. The more we can demystify who others are.

Possessing a strong sense of connectivity and engagement and involvement here I think allows us to bring the change that we are looking to bring or, at least, the exposure that we are looking to bring. This is where we have the opportunity to truly bring our cultures together at scale. To bring pride into that and to bring ownership of that and/or to secure and protect the ownership of that. I think media is probably one of the most important ways we can drive not just our coming together as a global community but the economics that fuel that coming together.

Everything in life is based on what you bring in and what you put out. It is integral to everything in life. And at the end of the day, you win when you bring in more than you put out every day. P&L (profit and loss) to me is kind of analogous to life. In a business setting, everything you need to know about a business's health, its ability to survive, and its ability to grow, you can determine from its P&L. Everything. This is where, especially in business, one of the things that I always hear about is that we (the Black community), are not often put in P&L roles in corporate America, and we're not often trained on the P&L statement—its purpose, importance, or even how to read it. As a result, our abilities to run businesses are limited, which is why we end up in corporate DEI roles or marketing roles instead of roles within the business that actually own the P&Ls. By the time you get to the head of marketing, I would expect that you would understand how to run a P&L. But in most of those organizations, marketing doesn't own the P&L; they just manage it. What that means is that the ability to invest back into the business or in the Black community comes from the Earnings Before Interest, Taxes, Depreciation, and Amortization (EBITDA).

This is what we are here to do. If we are running a business, we are here to maximize the EBITDA, because that EBITDA is what allows us to go back and invest in our communities and what allows us to invest in our people, our teams, our infrastructure, education, and healthcare. All the things that make a healthy community, that make a healthy business, are a result of how you manage that bottom line, how you manage the inputs and outputs so that you have what is necessary to drive and to grow. Because if there are more outputs than inputs, eventually you run out, and there is nowhere to go. So, for me, in business, this intense focus on the P&L with the outcome being maximizing the EBITDA is critical, because that is the only way I can invest back into my community. And as Emmet says, the revolution must be financed.

"The revolution must be financed," Emmet says. "It's a revolution of our purpose: Allowing people to live more beautiful lives, which means being able to support your family, having access to food, education, to live in whatever community you choose to." (Emmet Dennis in *The Philadelphia Citizen*.)

We cannot transform our communities if we don't have the capital to do it or if we are constantly asking somebody else for the capital to invest in our communities—you know, like, "Please give us this money so we can go administer it." How about let's make the money and let's operate the things that we need to operate in our community? So, yeah, P&Ls for me are at the central point of my being and certainly of our businesses. I'm obsessed with P&L.

Every job in corporate America has some sort of budget attached to it, so on the creative side, there is a creative budget. Someone will come to you and say, "Hey, Miss Creator, here is the budget for you to go create this video." Well, in my world, I would like to see Miss Creator say, "Okay, I want to understand how you came up with that budget. Help me understand all the things that went into that budget. Because at the end of the day, all the things that went into that budget will enable me to have enough to go do what I need to do. If it is not enough, I will have to scrape resources together to get there. Either way, that budget is what drives my career. That budget is what determines whether I'm able to create dope shit over a long period, or dope shit one time, or never create dope shit at all. Or create dope shit intermittently."

So, if someone comes to you with a budget, ask that person how they came up with that budget, because you need to understand it. You want to learn every component of the budget. And then when you get to the guy who's creating the budget, you're like, "Hey, how does this budget have an overall impact on all the things that we do in this business?" So it is not just me who gets the budget; it is me, the creative director; it is me, the videographer; it is me, the writer. All these budgets are coming from all over. At the end of the day, when you put all those budgets together, they are what make up the P&L inside of a company. It's not necessarily a numbers thing; while being good at numbers is helpful, it's merely understanding a breakdown of what goes in, what comes out, and what's left over. That is how I think about it. Always be curious about where the money is coming from. The good news is that there are all kinds of information and access online around P&Ls and how they operate. LinkedIn is a great resource (go to www .linkedin.com/pulse/simple-guide-understanding-your-profit-loss-statement-fastercapital/ for a Simple Guide to Understanding Your Profit and Loss Statement). There is a great deal of opportunity to go and educate yourself on that. Again, like I said earlier, ask questions and ask people around you. Identify people who are in these roles, those who are in the finance roles or the accounting roles, and ask them.

We run Essence Ventures with an entrepreneurial mindset. What we try to do is bring structure to the entrepreneurial mindset by implementing processes and procedures, and P&Ls are probably the number one driver of that. The process evolves from this intermediate place, where you're a start-up, then midsize, midtier, then you're scaling, and then you're growing. Start-up and growth are two very different stages, two very different types of activity. Going from growth to scale requires a different set of activities, different needs, and different skill sets. Where are we now with Essence in reality? Essence is a fifty-year-old brand in our community that feels big, but when you think about the overall media community, Essence is tiny. We have taken it back to the start-up phase to reset and retool all the components of the business so we can put it on a better footing to attain growth, and then we'll go from growing to scaling. What we are doing is resetting the infrastructure and the tools—or let us call it "the foundation"—so we can scale. We have been in this space for a few years now, but this allows us to build entrepreneurship into the infrastructure, because Essence had gotten to a—let us call it—growth stage, and then their move to scale was being acquired by Time Inc., and Time was supposed to bring that scale, which never happened.

A few of the things that should have been put in place to allow that scale to happen weren't put in place, or the things that were put in place to allow that scale to happen weren't adequate in allowing that scale to happen. We have pared it back down to "Hey, let us go redo the foundation here," and then from that, we can get to growth and then to scale. The idea is to build an infrastructure that allows Essence Ventures to scale, but for that to happen, these individual brands must have the right tools, the right resources, and the right teams, because that scale is going to come from the growth of those brands.

I think we are living the future. I think the future is transforming. We're in this start-up phase that we think we've got a good handle on, and we are getting ready to move into growth and then from there to scale. But what we are trying to ensure is that the generations that have been impacted and got their growth and their development from Essence feel proud about that heritage and that they feel connected to the future. We want the young folks who are now being introduced to Essence and haven't had that same history with it, to feel connected and inspired to push the journey for us. You know, we're now entering a world where Essence is no longer the one that determines what your experience is. Essence is now the one that facilitates you curating your own experience, and that is the difference.

Caroline and I are sort of figuring out how we can make that happen and how we can make that sustainable and exciting. This is the substance of the hundred-year plan. That's what we're building. We are building the hundred-year plan now, and then that's what we will hand off. The thing about building a hundred-year plan is that it probably won't be the plan that they will use twenty years from now, but what it will be is the guide and the discipline of thinking one hundred years out so that you're not caught flat-footed as you rotate, because just about every week we experience something new. Five years from now, two years from now, and one year from now, they might be changing that plan, because the world is changing so quickly. But what we are doing is creating the discipline so that our organization is structured with flexibility and has the mindset of being here for a hundred years and is therefore planning for that. That's the exciting part of what it is that we're doing. Today as we work, here's how we see the future. Tomorrow, the people who come behind us may see it differently, but let them at least have a plan as to where we were headed, the things that we saw, the things that we thought would be important to focus on, and they can then make those decisions. So, the handoff hasn't happened yet. Right now, we're still building, but that's the idea.

# Diasporic Disconnect

As a global brand, Essence recognizes the need to dismantle the barriers that Black folks around the world have erected among themselves and unite them for Global Black success. As we began to rebuild Essence and considered our passion for impacting Global Black, we were faced with the reality that there was and is much work to do. It begins with reconnecting the disconnected diaspora.

The division among Black folks is the stupid shit often being propagated by other Black folks. Examples include: colorism, Black elitism like the 1 percent foolishness, American-born Black versus other country–born Black, Black cancel culture, joy versus justice, and political divisiveness and corruption. I dare not give the groups that propagate this nonsense a centimeter of space in this book by naming them. However, there are three main themes to point out here. I mention them because, as with many successful African immigrants, I have come under fire for simply being who I am and having the audacity to thrive.

After Rich, who was born in Liberia, purchased Essence and put me, a Kenya-born immigrant, in place to run it, the noise was that we (the Africans) stole Essence from African Americans. Calls for boycotts and social media smears followed. Their attitude toward us was "Fuck those Africans. We don't need them. We'll build our own thing." Mind you, this noise came from "us," Black folks.

It's bullshit, but as of this writing it's legal, and that shit is working. The organizations that came for us at Essence are loud, but that did not make them right. Despite that, we are all connected. We are in this thing together. We need one another.

In *Things Fall Apart*, Chinua Achebe says "Until the lion learns how to write, every story will glorify the hunter."

Our efforts to reconnect the disconnected diaspora are grounded in the current realized opportunity for an ecosystem that economically equips the Global Black to regain its original wealth and thrive for several generations to come.

An example of that is what Vice-President Kamala Harris, US Secretary of State Tony Blinken, US Ambassador to Kenya Meg Whitman, and members of the US Congressional Black Caucus did during a summer of 2024 state luncheon in honor of President William Ruto of Kenya where they focused on rewriting outdated narratives about Africa.

President Ruto's remarks echoed a unified voice dedicated to shifting unregulated stories of a continent of disease, trouble, conflict, and poverty, to authentic identification of Africa as a continent of tremendous opportunity with the largest global reserves of renewable energy resources, 60 percent of the world's uncultivated land, and 30 percent of global mineral wealth. By 2050, with a current median age of nineteen, it will produce 40 percent of the world's workforce and 25 percent of the world's population will be living on the continent of Africa, therefore providing the world's largest single market.

In her remarks, Vice President Harris stated, "African ideas and innovations will have a significant impact on the future of the entire world." She recalled her weeklong trip to Africa last year (I was a part of the delegation) and how it informed her belief in the creativity, dynamism, and energy of young African leaders. It also fueled the need for a fresh focus on the ingenuity that is so prevalent across the continent of Africa.

This is why, across the ecosystem of the Sundial Group of Companies, we value connecting the disconnected diaspora. Whether it be the Global Black Economic Forum initiatives, our focused diasporic engagement efforts within Essence Ventures, or direct investments in African companies like Soko in Kenya, we aim to rewrite, rewire, and return value to what and who we are globally.

As a part of his opening remarks, Secretary Blinken referenced a quote by Benjamin Franklin that said "Well done is better than well said." Well, we'll see.

I gave a speech at the 2022 Essence Festival during the Black Women in Sports segment. I had just come off an encounter where someone informed me that everyone (there's that word) felt like Rich and me, as Africans, had stolen Essence from Black folks. Not gonna lie, it stung. There seemed to be a barrage and an amplification of this narrative in the two days before my speech. So when I got up to speak, I was emotional. I got through my address fine, but as I was wrapping up, I said this to the audience:

Something really simple that is a pet peeve of mine that I'm gonna put on the table, and then we're gonna shut up. All this about African versus US Black versus Caribbean Black versus Canadian Black versus Antarctica Black—I don't have facts to prove that. [Laughter.] We're everywhere! [Laughter.] If you allow that narrative to exist within you unregulated, you are participating in dismantling who we're supposed to be in the world, y'all. [Applause.] Rich and I are no less dedicated to the Black community in the US than we are to the Black community in Africa, the Caribbean, Europe, or anywhere else in the world. The fact that our collective descent is African in different ways doesn't mean we can't represent each other and fight for our collective needs and wants. But we keep accommodating a divisive narrative that impedes progress for all of us. Fucking—oops, sorry. [Laughter and applause.] I told y'all, this is me. If you called me on the phone, this is the way it would come out. I'm gonna tell you why I'm triggered by this in a second. Anybody can believe what they want to believe, but what I need you to do is proactively dismantle the part of the conversation that says, "If you weigh in on 'Black,' I certify that you [non-US Black] don't get to help make Black better." The amount of energy that we honestly spend trying to mitigate this is taking energy away from what we could be doing. I'm not ashamed to be Kenyan, and I am not ashamed that a big part of my life was lived in the US, but why do I have to sit there and think about this in an interview, on a stage, in public statements, in various other places where my primary responsibility is my work? Also, I gotta be careful about saying that I am from Kenya, because someone will think I can't lead them [or I don't care about them] because they're not from Kenya but they're Black like me. [I don't understand that.] The energy is, my Black can't be their Black, and their Black can't be my Black. So when I say "world," [I am saying] "all of us"! Spend that energy finding out what you can do. You don't gotta like me; you don't gotta think that I am gonna be successful. Just don't dismiss me because I'm Kenyan, and I won't dismiss you because you're [not]. If you are around people who are feeding the divisive narrative, believe you are obligated to tell them that they can feel how they want to feel, but please, don't force-feed that upon any-body, 'cause we all gotta work hard to eat, and the last thing that we need is our own folks in our way. Why am I triggered by that? Be-cause of the last two days and the next two days. [Do] you see how beautiful it is when we gather? [Do] you see what we've been able to do together unapologetically? Do you understand how this [being here at the festival] fuels them for when they have to go back and be "Black" where they came from? So what would the world look like . . . [Starting to cry.] What would it look like if we did this every day? We wouldn't need white people to save us. We'll take them as allies, but we wouldn't need them. So for those who are coming after us, as we honor these sisters [at this event] who have achieved so much in sports, I ask you to sit ever present in the me, we, us, and world mindset that should guide our collective efforts to succeed. That will truly get us to a place where the things that are thrown at us won't stick the same, because they're going to our back and not our front, because we're doing what we're supposed to be doing and standing where we are supposed to stand.

That audience was moved, as was demonstrated by their applause. But my heart was heavy. As a female CEO, particularly a Black female CEO, I am aware that I run the risk of being labeled too emotional, angry, or loud. I can't give a shit about that. I am emotional, I do get angry, and sometimes I am loud. I am also contemplative, empathetic, and resolute. There are variables within that spectrum that are subject to my authenticity and empower my success as a CEO, thought leader, and trailblazer.

After I gave that speech and call to action, the trolls of the internet, who shall not be named, found it on YouTube and clipped it perfectly to feed their narrative. Fortunately, their attempt to derail the message and discredit me didn't get much traction. In fact, people searched for the full speech and then understood the full context of the circumstances that led to my remarks. As with anybody whose role is public-facing, the more exposure you receive, the more justified folks feel in celebrating and desecrating you. It comes with the territory. So for the bulk of 2022, this noise around all of this us-and-them mentality got loud, personal, and threatening. As a result, Rich and I spent much of our time managing and mitigating. I can't change people's opinions of me, nor do I care to. When I give a speech, a personal quote, or a statement born out of an authentic moment in my life, I can't spend time worrying about whether someone will come along and weaponize it. I've got shit to do, and I refuse to give them any energy. But that doesn't mean I don't feel it. Dealing with publicity was always a part of my job description, but COVID shielded me from it in the beginning. When the world opened up again after the pandemic, I was fully exposed and visible to the public. So navigating publicity as an introvert was a challenging but necessary part of my day-to-day. I was now in the line of fire, and I couldn't hide behind the scandal or COVID. It became *Okay, Caroline. What are you gonna do? I'm gonna win, thrive, and grow this business. That's what the hell I'm gonna do.* Part of my external support and growth of Essence and me as a Black CEO was my participation in Black media executives uniting in support of one another. We began informally with the who's who of Black media. John Johnson and Eunice Johnson, cofounders of Johnson Publishing Company, and Earl Graves, founder and CEO of *Black Enterprise*, are all pioneers in the Black media industry. We all stand on the shoulders of these giants. When they were coming up, the bigotry and barriers to entry were deeply ingrained within corporate America. Ad dollars, product placement, and the distribution of their productions and publications were divvied out in ways that created a highly competitive space. There was no uniting in solidarity or collective bargaining, and honestly, back then, any attempt would likely have meant the demise of them all.

The year 2022 saw the rise of the new Black media leadership. It was me; Detavio Samuels, CEO of REVOLT TV; Jason Lee, CEO of Hollywood Unlocked; Morgan DeBaun, CEO of Blavity Inc.; Earl "Butch" Graves Jr., CEO of *Black Enterprise*; and Michelle Ghee, CEO of *Ebony*. Other than Butch, we didn't have a heritage relationship with the companies we represented, so there was nothing competitive among us to influence personal animosity. So we started to gather for quarterly lunches. While we were still competitors, when we met together, we were not as guarded as we might have been had we carried the weight of legacy. We pooled our interests and resources to support one another. Each of us owned an annual premier event, and we began to invite one another to them all. This is when I coined the word "co-opetition." As our bond became more visible, it pushed corporate America and sponsors into an uncomfortable position. Their narrative had always been

"There's only so much Black money" or "We can only support one of you," which was a song they were happy to keep singing, stanza after stanza, because that was the way it had always been. They had been comfortable. Our united front disrupted their comfort. As Detavio has said publicly, "If left to 'them,' we'd be left scrapping for a meager 1 percent of the advertising pie. But we've chosen defiance. We're banding together, unifying our voices, and setting our sights on the remaining 99 percent."

Our united front didn't automatically shift the old energy of corporate sponsors crying "broke." But what we did was use the rules of engagement to the benefit of the collective. If one of us went in and secured sponsorship, we would bring someone else to the table from our collective to secure sponsorship as well. We were positioning ourselves differently with the partners we normally competed for. We each maximized relationships with our existing corporate sponsors and encouraged new sponsors to look at each of us for engagement and support. The idea of banding together in a consortium, a Black media coalition, was something I championed very early on at Essence. But as my responsibilities increased, I pivoted to things within the organization that needed my immediate attention. Rich never forgot about it and cofounded Group Black, which disrupted the systems that were preventing Black media entities from getting revenue by making them a collective whose joint inventory increased access to capital. In 2023, the pendulum shifted, and the larger Black media companies went back to working together more informally, but the smaller Black media companies still functioned in partnership with Group Black. Much of the focus now was centered around the George Floyd fatigue. We would check in with one another to discuss its effects on our businesses. *How are your people? Are you seeing return-to-office fatigue? Are you losing money? Have you adjusted strategies? What are you doing for the emerging Latina/Latino and Afro-Latina/Latino markets?* At Essence, we were focusing the Afro-Latina energy into BeautyCon, and I was happy to share that with the group. It's more about support and conversations with folks who are walking similar paths. The corporate partners know we still communicate with one another. So if I go in and they tell me they've got twenty million to spend, then Detavio or Morgan go in and they can't secure five million, we're going to tell one another. Another way we support one another is to sit on panels for our respective events. I sat on a panel for the REVOLT Summit 2023, and Detavio asked me to answer a question explaining the difference between "Black-owned" and "Black-targeted." I talked about the importance of Black media companies ensuring that they're engaging in mutually beneficial partnerships that invest in Black consumers.

"This isn't about only Black people partaking in Black media, participating in Black culture . . . it can be for all. But you need to return the full value to the group that creates it. The problem with Black-targeted versus Black-owned is Black-targeted doesn't seed the ROI (return on investment) back to Black," I explained. "Every dollar you give VH1, BET . . . all of those dollars that go to non-Black-owned media companies do not come back to our community, do not create Black generational wealth, do not create a reality where economic inclusion is a human right. Those dollars go back to someone else.

"Everybody can participate in Black culture, but you must pay for it at its full value, and you must pay the culture that develops it. We have a saying at Essence that was started by one of our partners that is very simple: 'The revolution must be financed at full value, not discounts.'" I was pretty shocked at how many people didn't understand the difference. I contextualized it by giving the audience an inside look at how we handle our partnerships for Essence Fest.

"Our role is not just to bring money in via that festival and give it back to the community. What we also do with our presenting sponsors and others is, we not only have a sponsorship level with them, but within most of the contracts we have with our highest-level sponsors, we require that they hire Black businesses for how they show up at the festival, because if all they do is sponsor it, but the people that come and do their activation, the talent that they bring in . . . if all of that is not Black-owned, then the Black dollar stops at the point that it comes to Essence. When we say, 'If you're going to build an activation, you need to use a Black agency. If you're gonna create any sort of creative, you need to use a Black agency,' we don't tell them which agency to use; we tell them what dollar amount. So if you want to put your name on the highest, biggest festival in the country, then you gotta also commit to a certain amount of money for your activations going to additional Black business, or you can't have this slot. And so it's bigger than just the moment of the company."

The simple definition of "Black-owned," besides ownership, is "an unapologetic mission for Black." Reflecting on where I dedicate my time as CEO of Essence, I've noticed a tangible shift. There's now a greater proportion of my efforts, my voice, and our brand invested in educating corporate sponsors and fellow Black media outlets about the nuances distinguishing "Black-owned" from "Black-targeted." It is important to distinguish between the two, because knowledge of the differences informs so much of the ongoing narrative of "Black" in the marketplace and media. Consumer spending, branding, ad spending, allocation of outreach, efforts, social justice, and hiring practices. Earlier, when I talked about reconnecting the disconnected diaspora of Global Black, it was about a long-term strategy based on the Seventh Generation principle established by the Iroquois people. What is Seventh Generation thinking, and why is it important?

Seventh Generation thinking is about getting real with our impact. This is bigger than just checking boxes on environmental, social, and governance issues; it's about ensuring that our decisions don't just serve us now but build a legacy. It ain't just a concept; it's a call to action for the Global Black community. It's about handling the business of our business. It's about making sure that the way we grow our wealth, protect our planet, and uplift Global Black is on point. This ain't no five-year plan. We call it the hundred-year plan. This work is hard. The easy stuff you can get done in five years. But this ain't about quick wins. We're doing more than talking; we're laying the groundwork for a future where Black excellence is a given, not a fight. We're not interested in seeing it completed before we leave the planet. We just want to ensure that when we leave, we've left a succession plan and a solid structure that is better than when we found it. It's about making progress that our great-great-great-grandkids can run with and reap the benefits of.

In 2018, I was a few years into my authenticity journey, which, as I shared, was the basis for Rich thinking that I could go from

Target to running Essence. In 2018, Rich was at the end of one of the largest Black-owned beauty transactions in history and decided to step in and save Black media. I will remind you again that Rich and I did not meet until the summer of 2019. So for everybody who may think that my vision for *Essence* and Essence Ventures is simply the execution of Rich's dream, you're wrong. What is common between Rich and I is that we are two people who separately had clarity on our purpose in the world and had surrendered to this purpose on behalf of the greater good. My authenticity decisions were anchored in modeling what I wanted to be true for every person in the world. Rich's decisions on economic inclusion for all were anchored in his entrepreneurial pursuits and teaching those to anybody who wanted to learn. When our paths crossed, the timing was divinely ordered, and we had each already done the individual work to join forces and fight the obstacles to Black joy and Black justice. This is the intersection that Rich and I spend our time in. We don't aim to do the same thing or operate the same way; what we are aligned on is the destination.

I'm going to tell you a story that will hopefully help you understand this better. When Cadence was seventeen years old, she woke up and wanted grilled cheese. When I came downstairs, she had turned the toaster onto its side and had put two slices of bread and a slice of cheese in each slot. Why in the seventeenth year of her life she decided to make grilled cheese that way I will never know. What she did do was catch hell from me because of the impending fire hazard she was about to cause by ignoring all the tools that were available to make grilled cheese the way she had been taught. With an extended number of expletives, I took the time to let her know all the rules she had violated. We never came to an agreement and spent the rest of the day mad at each other. While I still believe I was right, the underlying story here is that Cadence had decided not to make a grilled cheese sandwich the way I had taught her to make a grilled cheese sandwich. I had the choice to simply allow her to make a grilled cheese sandwich her way while standing next to her or making a grilled cheese sandwich my way. Since I had the authority, I shut down her way. The reality is, the destination was a grilled cheese sandwich, with several right ways to get there. Therefore, what this story illustrates is how Rich and I work together. We have agreed on a destination focused on catalyzing wealth for Global *Black*. However, we allow ourselves to independently design pathways to that destination however we choose to. At the heart of this is why we work. We agree on the destination and negotiate the paths to get there. As long as the destination stays in sight, we don't manage each other's how. Rich and I have a hundred-year plan for Essence Ventures, and neither one of us is going to make it to a hundred years old; however, the destination will be a little bit closer when we finish our work, so the next "Rich" and the next "Caroline" will be able to pick up that baton and move it further ahead.

Before you say, "No, I did not sign up to pick up a baton," let me remind you that you are at this point in the book. If you bought this book just to get a quick hit of inspiration or to marvel at the media-worthy snippets of my life, and you ain't planning on doing a damn thing with it, then you've wasted your time—and mine. This ain't just about making Caroline better; it's about using my journey to propel you into action, to get you to step up and create a cycle of upliftment.

If you ain't ready to be as real, as raw, and as loud about the battles and victories of life, then you're failing. Not just yourself, but the generations to come. Because believe this—you ain't taking your self-improvement to the grave. The real test is what you leave behind for others, how you define your time here by how you've impacted those left standing when you're gone.

A hearse does not have a luggage rack. That means whatever you have done while you are here will stay here when you are gone. Whether you did anything while you are here will only be understood in how your legacy shows up in others. So if you spend your whole life working on yourself to be a better person, and the only person who is better because of it is you, then once you are gone, you will not have done anything. But if you take the steps to ensure that what you did to be a better person is intentionally shared with and embedded in the people around you and coming after you, then you go from a scenario of having done nothing to having done everything for everyone. Choose wisely.

I want to call upon your inner child to remember a book called *The Monster at the End of This Book*, which stars Grover from *Sesame Street*. The premise for the book is that Grover is becoming aware that there is a monster at the end of the book, and Grover is trying to convince the reader not to finish the book so that they do not encounter the monster. He spends several pages building obstacles to prevent the reader from reading further, but none of the obstacles work. Once Grover gets to the end of the book, he sees that the monster is himself. He laughs and pretends he knew that all along to cover the embarrassment regarding his fear of himself. Don't be Grover. FINISH. What I am saying here is, once you discover your purpose and you activate the pursuit of it, don't let anything stop you from fulfilling it. If you are scared, do it scared. If it's uncomfortable, push into the discomfort and do it anyway. If you feel alone, go by yourself. The thing you can't see on this side of your fear is that the universe will connect you with the partners, helpers, and opportunities you need to move forward. Peace and prosperity will arise out of your defiant pursuit of purpose, and you will do what you thought you couldn't do and land in spaces and places you have never dared to even dream that you could.

# #TakeNotesDoItBetter

Whether I knew it was intuition at the time, my life's journey has been guided by intuition. I did not always know the final destination; I just knew the next turn. I'm giving you permission to function the same way. In this chapter, I'm not asking you to document your life story or identify what you are going to get done before you die. I'm simply inviting you to participate in the path to purpose that is guided by the nudges of your intuition and your inner saboteur; those are the two most important voices for you to understand. One will guide you forward and positively; the other will always keep you stuck and negative. It is important that you understand the voice of each one so you are equipped to engage with each of them in alignment with what you are trying to create in service of your purpose. The more you practice courageously listening to these voices, the better you will become at enduring the presence of the saboteur and accelerating when your intuition is present, and that is how you win. Out of that, *I Am Highly Percent*

*Sure* that what you are about to write down will be exactly what you need to take the next step, even if it is not the final step. You now have a choice; once you write it down, decide if you believe that what you just wrote down will set a course that propels you to your purpose, or you can decide to challenge this philosophy, prove me a liar, and let me know that what I offered doesn't set any kind of course for you at all. The point is, write it down.

Godspeed.

# How Did You Get Here
# (In My Deborah Cox Voice)

I don't know if this can be attributed to a person or not, but there is a saying that is always on my mind that goes "Network your net worth." One of the things that I know has propelled my professional experiences has been relationships—more specifically, the capital associated with those relationships. I never planned to open a business; I opened a business to take in the money I had been offered. Very quickly, I realized that it would be in my best interest to legitimize the business so that the fees I was being offered would be properly managed. So to re-emphasize what I shared with you in earlier chapters, it was from fear of the IRS that Cadence and I recognized that we needed someone to help us set up our business the right way. As I thought through my network to see who could help, I remembered that a woman whom I worked with at Target was now operating a business helping people start businesses. So I connected her with Cadence, and from that day forward, she has been critical to how WangaWoman is built, operates, and adds value. WangaWoman LLC would not have happened without my friend La Juana Whitmore. La Juana is a business strategist, accredited small business consultant, university professor, and CEO of WangaWoman. She is passionate about helping businesses launch and grow. La Juana spent nearly twenty years with Target in business analysis, architecture, and strategy consulting, and she has advised hundreds of small firms and nonprofits. Upon leaving Target, she worked in nonprofit program delivery and administration as a business consultant, director of business solutions at Metropolitan Economic Development Association (MEDA), and executive director for the Jeremiah Program. La Juana holds a bachelor's degree in small business management and entrepreneurship and a master's degree in nonprofit administration, and is currently a business administration doctoral candidate exploring the effects of personality traits on the success of women entrepreneurs. La Juana's personal mission is to help entrepreneurs create wealth for their businesses, themselves, and their communities through entrepreneurship education and business development. Going back to what I said at the beginning of the paragraph, had I not leveraged my network and remembered what La Juana was doing that aligned with what was needed at the moment, the worth of WangaWoman would have been significantly diminished without her expertise and leadership. I stand forever grateful for my connection to her for how her purpose comes to life and how she has propelled mine.

I've asked La Juana to discuss career mapping. This isn't a how-to; she simply points us toward the definition, uses, value, and ideas for the creation of your career map.

## What Is a Career Map?

As a business consultant, I view a career map as a concise, personal business plan. It serves as the guide to navigating from your current position in your career to your desired destination. Just as with a business plan, it's crucial to not only envision the end goal but to also articulate your objectives and the strategies to achieve them. My suggestion is to visualize your future three to five years ahead. Consider where you want to be in your career, whether it's a specific role, title, company, or whatever it is—you have to see it first. Once you have a clear picture, the next step is to map out the necessary experiences and milestones, similar to what Caroline accomplished with her career map. This process is about identifying the essential experiences needed to reach your career goals.

### Where Do I Begin? (I Think the "Vision" Is the First Step [Outlined Above].)

The next step is about understanding the experiences you need to have to get where you want to go. This may include finding mentors, talking to folks in those roles, talking to your supervisor, or doing other research. Ultimately, there must be alignment between the experiences and the desired end.

### What Is the Next Step?

After that, it is about putting timing around each of those goals and experiences and then just start working the plan. That is the plan. It's funny, because it is very much like a business plan or a strategic plan that people want to overcomplicate. A plan is [simply] determining what you want to accomplish [based on your vision], determining the tactics needed, ensuring you've set a desired completion date, and finally deciding how you will measure it so you can definitively say,

"Yes, it is complete" or "No, it's not." These SMART (specific, measurable, achievable, relevant, and time-bound) goals are a great way to hold yourself accountable and move toward what you envision for your life.

### A Career Map Is Not an IDP and Not the Norm

A few things that were interesting about the Target experience: I worked at Target for almost twenty years, and so one of the many things that Target did well was that they gave you the language to talk about what you were good at and what you needed to work on, and then described behaviors that would help you either capitalize on your strengths or mitigate your (what we called) opportunities, not weaknesses. What we used to manage those conversations was called an individual development plan (IDP). You and your boss would use the IDP to assess how you were demonstrating the behaviors needed to be considered doing your job well or how you were maybe even ready for promotion. It was not much more future-looking than twelve months (if that). The IDP was normal, but it was not a career map.

Caroline took those concepts a few steps further. What was not common was for people to create an individual career map, which is what Caroline did. I don't know of anyone else who had a formal, individual career map that helped describe where they wanted to be in the organization several years down the road.

### How?

Again, if you want to do this, one thing that would be helpful is to talk to people and find out what experiences you need to get to this place that you want to be in. If you want to be the vice president of D&I, what do you need to do to make sure that you get there? If you want to be a senior group HR manager or, even more generically, if you want to lead people, what types of experiences do you need to have to ensure you get the opportunity to lead people? It's one thing for you to create this plan in a silo on your own, but if other people don't agree that the objectives listed on your career map are indeed the things that are going to get you where you want to go, then they may not have the impact you desire.

## Why Do I Need a Career Map?

Most people should create a career map. The power of writing down your goals (and looking at them) has been studied. But what's also powerful about the career map is having it on hand as a way to facilitate conversations with people who can help you. So as you're going around and talking to people who can help you identify or define the behaviors or experiences you need to accomplish your plan, it ends up building your network of people who can speak on your behalf, which is often more powerful than speaking for yourself.

## Planning and Organization

I think the career map needs to be organized, but it doesn't have to be that beautiful; it needs to be functional. I know that there are people who love templates, and I'm a template girl myself, but what I often say is that what's going to work is what you're actually going to use. So if it's an Excel spreadsheet, if it's a Word document, if it's a PowerPoint page, whatever is going to work is what you're going to use. If you don't like Excel, for God's sake, don't put it in Excel.

## Final Thoughts from the CEO

I am a big advocate of planning. It's really hard to get where you want to go without a plan.

# My Petty Pahtnas

We have all experienced particular people in our lives who just jive with who they naturally are. So whether you call them "petty pahtnas," aka "my tribe," aka "my chosen family," you get it.

These are some of mine.

I am Lauretta P. Moore. The *P* stands for *PZ*! 😄 I'm Caroline's bestie—three decades and holding—and the gatekeeper of skeletons and all things secret and sacred to this sisterhood!

Whether Caroline is laser-focused on self-preservation or a task that will undoubtedly incorporate the ability to sow seeds in others, humility and intentionality will always be her portion! Caroline is a whimsical whirlwind. A cornucopia of customized contradictions that accentuate the Creator's obvious freehand design when she was fearfully and wonderfully crafted in Mama Wanga's womb to positively shift or enhance any atmosphere.

## LPM
*Caroline's Friend*


We have a book filled with African proverbs in our heads—catch it when you catch it. One is to listen with your eyes. 👀 During Essence Fest, when the social capital hits its highest, she starts to speak Liberian. Ummm, she's not Liberian, and the laughers are the fuel that follows and keeps the energy going. And she's a hater of my greatest accomplishment of being Africa's most famous social influencer. And at any given moment, she can be heard saying about me, "I love her, but I don't like her." She's verbose and not working on it. 💁

## Barkue Tubman
*Caroline's # 1 Life Bully*


Caroline and I met in our twenties. We had too much fun while figuring out life, most of which will never be discussed. When I reflect, I think, *Look how far she's come*, and then I quickly think, *She has always been Caroline—brilliant, inspiring, and trendsetting.*

## Chanda Smith Baker
*Caroline's Friend*


Lord help me. This lady, my little sister, my friend. My family is hers, and her family is mine forever. All the people she brought with her belong to me as well. I love that crazy, funny, smart, motivating soul that I sometimes call Wangstine. I can sum her up in one word: LOVE!!!! I love her, she loves me, it's Real Love. Here is a funny inside truth. After church one Sunday, Caroline, Lauretta,

Peggy, and I sat around my dining room table, as we often did. My Holy Rollie behind got on their nerves as I was praying and being deacon of the world. Things got real silly, and we ended up co-founding a club we named Shake-a-Tail-Feather Ministries. Our mission was to allow us to talk freely and stay saved as we explored our stripper ambitions. The first order of business was to pick your name, then your theme song, and then your loyalty. I'll keep everybody else's answers private, but I'll share my name and theme song. My chosen name was Coco Chanel, and my song was "How Do U Want It" by Tupac. From that moment on, this is how we would always giggle while serving the Lord. Although the ministry is no longer active because we had to grow up and do adult things, it still lives within each of us, and we still refer to one another by our chosen names. I love her to the moon and back, period . . .

## Ruby Brown
*Caroline's Friend*

# A Note on the Cover Design

To me, intuition is a deep trust not only in yourself, but in the abilities you've been given. Everything about this piece was based on a trust and faith that what needed to be would be. To create "Intuition," I cut on music that made me feel deeply. Music with no words, but a large amount of emotion. I didn't think about what I was creating as much as I felt what I was creating. I went into the process blindly, no planning, no revisions, just raw emotion painted onto a canvas for whoever would see it. The absence of color allowed for my mind to run free without pressure. The conclusion of this piece left me almost in tears as I realized the pressure I would normally feel to create did not exist in this space. I was able to just be, to just vent and scream on a canvas what was already placed within me.

*LaKendra Huckaby*

# ABOUT THE AUTHOR

Caroline A. Wanga is the president and CEO of Essence Ventures. She joined as chief growth officer in 2020 after a fifteen-year career at the Target Corporation, where she started as an intern and held a number of transformational leadership roles, eventually serving as Target's chief diversity, inclusion, and culture officer. Prior to Target, she spent almost a decade in youth and community development at several nonprofit organizations in the Minneapolis–St. Paul area.

In 2020, she cofounded WangaWoman LLC, whose mission is to "democratize authenticity." A self-proclaimed cultural architect who refers to her personal style as armor, Caroline's "real talk" delivery and unmitigated perspective make her a highly sought after keynote speaker, equity strategist, thought leader, and community adviser/influencer.

Caroline serves on several corporate advisory boards and has received numerous awards, accolades, and honors, including the National Action Network's Keepers of the Dream Award and two honorary doctorate degrees, one from her alma mater, Texas College, and another from Dillard University. She is a Kenyan citizen and her greatest accomplishment in life is her daughter, Cadence.